Lernthriller Englisch

FACELESS KILLER

Vanessa Vollmann

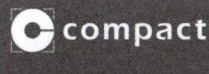

Weitere Informationen zu Compact Lernthrillern finden Sie am Ende des Buches und unter www.lernkrimi.de.

© Compact Verlag GmbH
Baierbrunner Straße 27, 81379 München
Ausgabe 2012

Chefredaktion: Dr. Matthias Feldbaum
Redaktion: Helga Aichele
Fachkorrektur: La Kenya Houston
Produktion: Johannes Buchmann
Titelabbildung: fotolia.com, Andrey Bortnikov
Lernkrimi-Logo: Carsten Abelbeck
Gestaltung: EKH Werbeagentur Gbr, textum GmbH
Umschlaggestaltung: EKH Werbeagentur Gbr, Hartmut Baier

ISBN 978-3-8174-8856-8
381748856/1

www.compactverlag.de, www.lernkrimi.de

VORWORT

Liebe Leserin, lieber Leser,

mitreißend und unheimlich spannend – die Compact Lernthriller mit ihrer Kombination aus fesselnder Lektüre und didaktischem Übungsanteil eignen sich hervorragend, um breite Sprachkompetenzen in der Fremdsprache zu erwerben. Der Lerner wird dabei durch die atemberaubende Handlung, das angemessene Sprachniveau und den stetig ansteigenden Schwierigkeitsgrad der Übungen gefördert und motiviert. Ein ausführlicher Abschlusstest ermöglicht das Wiederholen und Festigen des Gelernten. In einem alphabetischen Glossar am Ende des Buches sind noch einmal übersichtlich alle Vokabeln zum Nachschlagen aufgelistet.

So lernen Sie mit Compact Lernlektüren:
• **Mit Begeisterung lernen:** Die packende Handlung motiviert Sie beim Lesen des englischen Originaltextes.
• **Wissen intensivieren und erweitern:** Durch die Kombination aus didaktisierter Lektüre und textbezogenen Übungen testen und trainieren Sie Ihre Sprachkenntnisse effektiv. Vokabelangaben auf jeder Seite unterstützen Sie beim Lesen.
• **Systematisch lernen:** Knüpfen Sie an Ihr individuelles Sprachniveau an und setzen Sie eigene Lernziele – linear im Schwierigkeitsgrad ansteigend oder mit punktuellen Schwerpunkten von Grundwortschatz bis Hörverstehen.
• **Unabhängig sein:** Lernen Sie ganz individuell – wo und wann Sie wollen.

Viel Spaß beim **spannend Englisch lernen**
wünscht Ihnen

Prof. Dr. Christiane Neveling
Didaktik der romanischen Sprachen, Universität Leipzig

INHALT

ZU DIESEM BUCH

Auf der Suche nach ihrem spurlos verschwundenen Vater fliegt die junge Penelope nach Atlanta. Dort wird sie in eine Serie mysteriöser Todesfälle verstrickt: Mehrere Bekannte ihres Vaters sterben qualvoll vor ihren Augen. Und auch Penelope selbst gerät durch ihre Nachforschungen bald ins Visier des Killers. Es beginnt ein Wettlauf gegen die Zeit ...

Die Ereignisse und die handelnden Personen in diesem Buch sind frei erfunden. Etwaige Ähnlichkeiten mit tatsächlichen Ereignissen oder lebenden Personen wären rein zufällig und unbeabsichtigt.

1 THE ATLANTA CONNECTION

Penelope pushes the heavy metal door open and steps into her father's hothouse. This first step into her father's universe has always been special to her. The smell of so many orchids is just wonderful. It's a smell that reminds her of her own childhood and still makes her heart feel light today as a grown woman. She can almost feel her father's presence.

hothouse	Gewächshaus
orchid	Orchidee
to glimpse	flüchtig erblicken
rocking chair	Schaukelstuhl
award-winning	preisgekrönt

It's still early – only eight o'clock in the morning, but today she has no time to stop and enjoy the moment. She is breathing hard after running through her father's house before coming here into the garden. This is it. This is the last place he can be...

"Father," she calls.

She doesn't get an answer. "Father?"

This time her voice is louder and stronger. She continues walking through the hothouse, checking everywhere. Right at the back, she glimpses the rocking chair that he sits in every evening before he wishes his orchids good night.

She turns around and notices her father's newest award-winning orchid. The flower bed is dry. He never leaves his plants like this.

These plants are very **valuable** and need almost as much care and attention as little children.

Penelope feels her heart grow cold. Where is he? Something is wrong. She needs to stay calm and think carefully.

Penelope's father's neighbor called her late last night and told her that she had a parcel for her father. Penelope had asked why the neighbor had not already rung the doorbell and dropped off the parcel. The neighbor had answered that Penelope's father hadn't been in his house for the past two days.

valuable	wertvoll, kostbar
private	*hier*: zurückhaltend
clue	Hinweis
to sweep	fegen
rocker	*hier*: Kufe
flight attendant	Stewardess

Her father is a very **private** person and doesn't have many close friends, only a few golfers and his colleagues. Penelope called two of his golfing friends, and they had no idea where he could be. Both her father's colleagues hadn't picked up the phone, so Penelope had left messages on their answering machines.

Penelope's mother died when she was only eight years old. Ever since then, they have been very close. Her father never leaves London without telling her where he is going. He is usually so thoughtful and even now, twenty years after her mother's death, they still speak on the phone every second day.

Now it's been three days since she has heard from him, so she has come to his house to search for him. She went through his mail and made sure that her father hadn't left a message on the answering machine. She even checked if a suitcase was missing, but she found nothing. There were no **clues** that her father was planning to leave.

Should she call the police? Has something happened to him – maybe an accident?

Exercise 1: Match up the phrases. Welche der folgenden Wendungen gehören zusammen? Ordnen Sie zu!

1. ☐ to feel   **a)** a parcel

2. ☐ to drop off   **b)** the doorbell

3. ☐ to go   **c)** someone's presence

4. ☐ to ring   **d)** through the mail

Penelope shakes her head and runs her fingers through her hair in frustration. She is listed as his emergency contact, but the police haven't called her. So there probably hasn't been an accident. But why has he left his plants? Why hasn't he called her?

Still shaking her head, she turns around and sweeps some dust off the cushion on the rocking chair. The cushion falls to the floor, and Penelope bends to pick it up. She notices a little piece of paper sticking out from under one of the rockers.

It is an empty envelope. She turns it over and sees something that surprises her. On the front of the envelope she recognizes her father's handwriting. It says:

Judy Harrington – Valley Road Atlanta, GA 30305, April 29th – BABG – 001 404 555 1996

Three hours later, Penelope turns around to the flight attendant who approaches her in the VIP Lounge of Heathrow Airport.

"Miss? We are boarding now. Can I ask you to come with me?"

Penelope realizes that she is the only one left sitting in the lounge. Everyone else has already started boarding the plane to Atlanta. She is happy that she has a Delta Sky Club card and can fly first class on short notice.

Penelope feels as if the whole day has already gone by, although it's only 11 o'clock in the morning here in London. From the moment she started looking for her father, so much has happened.

"Yes. Sorry. I was just thinking…," she says.

Penelope wants to add something, but the flight attendant has already walked on and isn't listening to her.

She desperately wants to let someone know about her plans to fly to Atlanta. But she can't call Ms. Harrington, because 11 o'clock in London is 6 o'clock in the morning in Atlanta. Right now, she needs a good piece of advice. Is it a good idea to fly to Atlanta without knowing anyone there? Her thoughts are so scattered.

desperately	verzweifelt
piece of advice	Ratschlag
scattered	*hier*: wirr
stopover	Zwischenstopp
to clench sth.	etw. (fest) umklammern
almond-shaped	mandelförmig
jet-black	pechschwarz
looks *pl*	Aussehen
to make a mental note to…	versuchen, daran zu denken zu …
sophisticated	kultiviert

Penelope gets up in a hurry, pulling her carry-on suitcase behind her. In her right hand, she is holding the letter her father left in the hothouse.

Ten minutes later, she is sitting in her first class window seat. This flight to Atlanta is not perfect because there is a stopover in Amsterdam. But it's the first and only daytime flight out of Heathrow. She has a strong feeling that it is important for her to get to Atlanta as soon as she can. Penelope's hand is clenching the envelope so tightly that her fingers hurt.

She looks out of the airplane window and sees her reflection. With her green, almond-shaped eyes and jet-black long hair, Penelope knows she has a face that many people say is beautiful, although she has never thought of herself in that way. And today, Penelope's looks are the last thing on her mind.

The flight attendant says that they are now ready for takeoff and asks all passengers to turn off their cell phones. Penelope makes a mental note to remember to call Ms. Harrington when she arrives in Amsterdam.

The pilot starts up the engines. Penelope normally feels very excited when she is traveling on business for the art gallery. Today, she only feels worried.

Exercise 2: Unscramble. Bringen Sie die Buchstaben in die richtige Reihenfolge!

1. chordi _____

2. lubevala _____

3. gasseme _____

4. felautibu _____

5. lopeneep _____

6. yercengem _____

Two hours later, in the Amsterdam airport transfer area, she finally dials Ms. Harrington's number. She just has to know who this Ms. Harrington is and about her connection to her father.

"Hello?" says a sophisticated American woman's voice on the third ring.

"Yes, hello. Am I speaking to Ms. Harrington?" asks Penelope.

"That would be me, honey. What exactly is it that you are calling about?"

Ms. Harrington has a strong, smoky voice. It is not hard at all to hear the slow **Southern** stretching of **vowels** [i] in every word she says.

"Yes, Ms. Harrington, how do you do? My name is Penelope Battersea, and I will be landing in Atlanta later this evening. I am looking for my…"

Penelope is interrupted by Ms. Harrington.

"Did you just say, 'How do you do?' How very British of you. I like the way you speak, you sound just like your daaaddy…"

Penelope raises her eyebrows in surprise. When Ms. Harrington says 'like', the sound she makes is 'laaaak'. And 'daddy' is such an American word.

"Yes, well…", **stutters** Penelope.

She is very surprised to hear that Ms. Harrington knows her father.

She takes a deep breath and continues, "I would very much like to speak to you as soon as I can, maybe tomorrow? But first I would like to ask you if you could suggest a hotel so I can make a reservation for a few nights? That would be very kind of you."

Southern	*hier*: aus den Südstaaten der USA
vowel	Vokal
to stutter	stottern
⚡ I'll have none of it.	Davon will ich nichts wissen.
⚡ Ya hear?	Verstehst du?
⚡ no buts about it	da gibt es kein Wenn und Aber
GACC (German American Chamber of Commerce)	Deutsch-Amerikanische Handelskammer
annual	jährlich
asparagus	Spargel

"Daaahlin', **I'll have none of that** hotel business for you, **ya hear**? I'll just have Bartholomew – that's maa driver – pick you up from the airport, and we'll have you over here in no time. **No buts about** it. You can stay on at maa place for just as long as you want. What airline did you say you are flying with?" asks Ms. Harrington.

"Ahhhm. Delta from Amsterdam, arriving in Atlanta at… hold on… let me check… yes, here it is… 8:20 p.m.," says Penelope while searching for her flight details.

"Bartholomew? Aah need you to pick up a lovely young lady from the airport this evening at 8:20, okay?" Penelope hears Ms. Harrington tell Bartholomew who is obviously standing somewhere nearby.

"That's settled then. See you this evening, sugar. Bartholomew will take you straight to the GACC's annual Asparagus Dinner and we'll talk there," Ms. Harrington says and hangs up.

With that, Penelope is left waiting at the Amsterdam airport with more questions than ever.

Exercise 3: Questions about the text. Beantworten Sie die Fragen zum Text in ganzen Sätzen!

1. Does Penelope's father have many friends?

   _____

2. Does Penelope know Ms. Harrington?

   _____

3. Is Penelope British or American?

   _____

4. What is Penelope's father's hobby?

   _____

There is, however, one bit of information that the search engine on her smart phone can help her with: what is this GACC that Ms. Harrington is talking about?

Ah yes, here it is. GACC is the German American Chamber of Commerce. So maybe Ms. Harrington is some kind of a professional person who works for them?

After arriving seven hours later in Atlanta, Penelope is exhausted. Atlanta must be the only airport in the world where you have to identify your luggage twice. Even traveling lightly with only a carry-on suitcase is not easy. Luckily, her ESTA documents are still valid from the last time she visited the US.

At last, Penelope is waiting in the main airport terminal with her suitcase and purse. She is hungry, confused, tired and worried, all at the same time. What time is it anyway? She looks for a clock. Ah, yes, there's one. It's 9:30 p.m. And standing over there it seems, is also Bartholomew.

exhausted	erschöpft
ESTA (Electronic System for Travel Authorisation)	Elektronisches Reisegenehmigungssystem der USA
valid	gültig
purse *US*	Handtasche
⚡ in no taam *US (Dialekt)*	sofort
expressway *US*	Schnellstraße, Autobahn
screen	*hier*: Trennscheibe
signature	*hier*: unverkennbar
headquarters	Zentrale

Penelope walks over to the tall, slightly-overweight African-American chauffeur, who is carrying a sign over his head with her name on it.

"Ma'am, call me Bartholomew, and might aah say that it's a real pleasure to meet you," he tells her when she introduces herself. "Aah've come to bring you to Miss Judith's. Please follow me to the limousine and aah will make sure you get there in no taam."

'Taam' probably means time, thinks Penelope.

She is really not used to being addressed as a 'ma'am' and feels a little out of place here with her British accent. She also really doesn't know what to say to Bartholomew. So she decides to not say anything at all and wait until she finally meets Ms. Harrington. Driving into Atlanta on the expressway, Penelope looks out of the limousine's window. Bartholomew has put up the screen between the driver's seat and the passengers' area.

Exercise 4: Verb forms. Ergänzen Sie Simple Past und Past Participle der folgenden Verben!

1. bring   _____   _____

2. leave   _____   _____

3. know   _____   _____

4. think   _____   _____

5. see   _____   _____

"This is what it must feel like to be really rich," says Penelope to herself and settles into the comfortable leather seat with a cold drink from the limousine's bar in her hand.

Outside, she sees the Atlanta skyline. On a tall building she recognizes the signature letters of the Coca-Cola logo. That must be the company's headquarters.

Although she is still worried about her father, she is excited to be in a new place – how she just loves traveling.

Maybe, she thinks, this is all just a big misunderstanding and Ms. Harrington will have some answers that explain her father's disappearance.

Thirty minutes later, the limousine pulls up in front of a **fancy-looking** restaurant in the glamorous Buckhead neighborhood in uptown Atlanta. Bartholomew opens the limousine door for her and tells her that he will be taking her luggage 'home' later.

Home? thinks Penelope, but she doesn't say it out loud. Somehow the impressions of the last few hours have left her **speechless**. A handsome doorman greets her at the entrance of the restaurant and asks to hang up her coat.

Penelope is standing in a very stylish, modern bar area that is connected to a dining room just a few

fancy-looking	schick
speechless	sprachlos
bank	*hier*: Ufer
to mill about	umherlaufen
bad con-science	schlechtes Gewissen
to eavesdrop	(heimlich) lauschen

feet away. From there, she realizes that the restaurant is located on the **banks** of what must be the Chattahoochee River which she read about on the Internet. Penelope is surprised at how hungry she is. But she also needs to find Ms. Harrington, so finding something to eat is not a priority.

There are about eighty people **milling about** and speaking to each other excitedly. The topic of the day seems to be a death.

In der 1901 gegründeten **Junior League** engagieren sich in den USA, Kanada und Mexiko v. a. wohlhabende Frauen für wohltätige Zwecke.

Penelope hears little phrases about a 'Josh' and a 'Mr. Duvane' and something about the 'Junior League' **i**. With a **bad conscience**, she realizes that she shouldn't be **eavesdropping**. However, she can't, stop herself from listening to the people talking.

Before she can ask someone about Ms. Harrington, Penelope notices a woman approaching her. The woman is about Penelope's father's age, in her late fifties or early sixties.

Ms. Harrington must have been very beautiful when she was younger, thinks Penelope, and she has aged well.

Although the woman's eyes seem very friendly, the look in them is careful. Penelope has the impression that the woman is masking another emotion – is she in some kind of pain?

"You must be Penelope," says the lady with the same voice that Penelope remembers from the telephone.

"How lovely it is to finally meet you," Ms. Harrington continues. "I've known your father for so many years now. Why, you look exactly like your daddy!"

Before Penelope can reply, Ms. Harrington adds, "Listen, daahling. You'll have to excuse me. Aah have a lot of guests here tonaat, but I want you to feel comfortable. Please call me Judy."

She gives Penelope a friendly smile.

"Aah understand that you need to speak to me, but there will be time for that later. Let's get you something to eat first, and aah will introduce you to some people."

"Uh, Ms. Harrington… ma'am…"

"Aah said, please call me Judy, young lady. Come on over here and let me introduce you to maa very good friend, Mrs. Carmine. She has come all the way from Covington tonaat just to have German asparagus here at our Junior League-GACC dinner," says Ms. Harrington. "Please meet the lovely Penelope."

Exercise 6: Adjectives. Lesen Sie weiter und unterstreichen Sie alle sieben Adjektive!

Mrs. Carmine holds out her small hand, and Penelope shakes it. Mrs. Carmine is about forty and appears very athletic; she has a thoughtful air about her. She is dressed in an old-fashioned cocktail dress and high heels. Although the dress has seen better days, Mrs. Carmine's outward appearance is nevertheless very attractive.

"Mr. McGraw here is a good friend, who also manages all the Junior League legal issues. Aah don't know where we would be without him," Ms. Harrington says, throwing him a smile that makes her decades younger.

Mr. McGraw nods to Ms. Harrington, obviously enjoying the compliment. He is the personification of a very successful lawyer, Penelope notices. He is impeccably groomed. The suit he is wearing was obviously expensive, just like his shoes. He must be about fifty and seems quite fit.

Penelope looks over to Ms. Harrington again. She has a spectacular smile, Penelope decides.

Then she sees Ms. Harrington's hand go to her stomach and her face cringe in pain.

And suddenly, Ms. Harrington is lifted up into the air. For just a moment she seems to fly. She opens her eyes in surprise, and in spite of her obvious pain, she laughs happily when she sees who it is.

"Oh Tommy, you old fool. How many years will you still be lifting me up like that," she exclaims.

They hug and the young man

air	*hier*: Ausstrahlung
lawyer	Rechtsanwalt
impeccably groomed	tadellos gepflegt
to cringe	(zusammen-)zucken
longish	ziemlich lang
facial features *pl*	Gesichtszüge
gesture	Geste
stage name	Künstlername
to glance	blicken

plants a kiss on her cheek. He has longish dark-brown hair and is very good-looking. He must be in his mid-thirties, but his facial features seem a little older, Penelope thinks when she comes closer to him. His manner is that of a true Southern gentleman. He takes Penelope's hand in a gallant gesture and kisses it.

"And you are?" he asks Penelope in a low voice.

"May I introduce Mr. Berger? Tommy – this is Penelope Battersea, from London."

"The pleasure's all mine," Mr. Berger replies. "But my friends call me Tommy. Tommy 'The Voice' Berger. That's my stage name."

Tommy glances around. He is obviously the type of man who loves to hear himself speak which is exactly the type of man Penelope can do very well without. What she needs now is a good excuse to go and talk to someone else. But Tommy does her the favor of turning away first. He leads Mr. McGraw away from the little group, talking to him excitedly. He has become very upset and keeps turning back to the group of people Penelope is standing with.

Suddenly, Penelope feels a cold object being placed in her hand. But before she can look at it, something hits her between her ribs, and she is gasping for breath. What is going on? What is happening?

Still breathing with difficulty, she realizes that Ms. Harrington has collapsed into her arms. Was it Ms. Harrington's head that struck her rib cage? Frightened and shocked, Penelope tries to pull Ms. Harrington into an upright position. But she can't.

She glances around and notices that Mrs. Carmine has stepped back, her face frozen. Mr. Berger is holding on to Mr. McGraw's arm. His other hand is covering his mouth, as if to silence a scream.

"Help me! For God's sake, help me!" yells Penelope.

Everyone reacts at the same time. It's as if the first shock has worn off and people have realized that they have a serious emergency on their hands. Mr. McGraw helps Penelope to lay Ms. Harrington down on the floor. Her eyes are closed. Penelope kneels down and holds her ear to Ms. Harrington's mouth. She is not breathing.

"Someone call an ambulance!" she hears a voice shouting through the room and people start running about.

"Is there a doctor here?" screams Penelope.

"Right here, young lady. Let me take over," says a man calmly.
Penelope's head is spinning as she watches the doctor resuscita-
ting Ms. Harrington. A few min-
utes later, she sees the ambulance
arrive. A whole group of paramedics is gathered around Ms. Harrington's body, trying to revive her.
What feels like hours later, the
doctor lifts up his head and says in
an exhausted voice, "I'm so sorry.
There was nothing we could do."
Then he looks at his watch. "Time
of death 22:34."
Penelope opens her fist, only now

to gasp for breath	nach Luft schnappen
rib cage	Brustkorb
frozen	*hier*: erstarrt
to resuscitate	wiederbeleben
to revive	(wieder)beleben
UCLA (University of California, Los Angeles)	Universität von Kalifornien
class ring	Absolventenring

realizing that she is still holding the object that Ms. Harrington put
there before she collapsed.
She is holding her father's UCLA class ring.

Exercise 8: Hidden words. Finden Sie im Gitternetz
sechs Wörter, die mit Reisen zu tun haben!

S	T	O	P	O	V	E	R
D	A	O	L	E	A	H	X
W	K	P	A	W	E	O	D
L	O	U	N	G	E	T	E
R	O	U	E	G	F	E	R
J	E	T	L	A	G	L	I
T	R	A	N	S	F	E	R

2 INCOGNITO

Penelope rubs her eyes. Her head is hurting, her throat is dry and she feels disoriented. She usually wakes up to the sound of her alarm clock to go jogging every morning at 5:30. Sport is very important to her; her friends always say that she is something of a jogging junkie.

Now as she sits up in bed, her body feels stiff. It takes her a second to realize where she is. This awful feeling must be jetlag. She tries to find the glass of water that Ms. Harrington's housekeeper placed on her bedside table last night.

"Ms. Harrington!" exclaims Penelope with a jolt.

She is wide awake now.

Ms. Harrington is dead. After the ambulance had taken her body away last night, Penelope just sat there in the spot in which Ms. Harrington's body had lain. A woman had died in her arms. Penelope can still feel the horror of Ms. Har-

jolt	*hier*: Schock
dreadful	fürchterlich
mansion	Villa
striking	auffallend
pillar	Säule

rington falling into her arms and then not breathing. How dreadful that had been.

Mr. McGraw had been the first person to take action after the doctor had announced Ms. Harrington's death. He had notified the police and arranged for Bartholomew to take Penelope to Ms. Harrington's house.

Penelope remembers how she looked out of the window of Ms. Harrington's limousine when they entered the driveway last night. This is no ordinary house, she had thought. This is a **mansion**. The **striking** white **pillars** in front of the huge front door had left a strong impression. She had practically expected Scarlett O'Hara to walk out of the mansion being escorted by Rhett Butler. The whole setting was one hundred percent 'Gone with the Wind'.

Exercise 9: Missing nouns. Lesen Sie weiter und ergänzen Sie die fehlenden Substantive!

staircase	breakfast	knock	kitchen	shower

voice

Her thoughts are interrupted by a **1.**   .

"Miss?" says a **2.**   quietly.

"Yes, please come in," answers Penelope.

"Oh no, miss, I wouldn't. I just wanted to know if you would like to have **3.**   this morning?"

"Oh... ahem... yes, thanks. Breakfast sounds good. I'll be right down," stutters Penelope.

Fifteen minutes later, she has taken a **4.**   and is walking down the winding **5.**   in search of the **6.**   .

She realizes that the servants probably think she will have breakfast in something like a dining room. But the last thing Penelope wants today is to eat by herself. She needs company.

After yesterday's horrible events, she is more desperate than ever to find her father. She needs to talk to someone about his disappearance.

Following the aroma of fresh coffee, she finds the kitchen. Penelope stops at the door and **clears her throat** after she sees someone standing by the stove talking to Bartholomew. She is a Caucasian [i] **plump**, middle-aged woman with a friendly smile, holding a **kettle**.

This is probably the cook, Penelope thinks. She must already know of Ms. Harrington's death.

Caucasian bedeutet hier nicht, dass die Köchin aus dem Kaukasus stammt. Der Begriff wird im Amerikanischen Englisch als Synonym für „white" verwendet und bezeichnet Amerikaner europäischer Abstammung.

"Good morning," says Penelope, feeling extremely uncomfortable. "Can I just say, I am very sorry for your loss."

Bartholomew and the cook look to her and say nothing.

"Please may I have some coffee?" Penelope asks.

The cook nods and says with a friendly voice, "Well, **chile**. Just set yourself right on down, and we'll get you a coffee just as fast as can be. And then we'll **sort out** the rest."

But before Penelope can sit down, she hears a loud banging noise.

That must be the front door, she thinks.

Then Penelope hears someone running to answer the door and a moment later someone shouting.

"COOK! It's the police. They've come to take us all to the police station. Us and the Miss Battersea that is stayin' with us. Standard procedure."

Exercise 10: Plurals. Bilden Sie die Pluralform!

1. woman _____

2. child _____

3. disappearance _____

4. door _____

5. voice _____

"Quit your **hollerin'**, chile," the cook replies. "Tell them cops to give us a minute. We be finishin' our coffee first, then we'll get ourselves to the police."

With that, she hands Penelope her coffee. Penelope nods a thank-you and puts on a brave face.

Oh, how I wish I could find my father, she thinks. Why did Ms. Harrington have his ring in her hand? Is this something I will have to tell the police? What is her father's connection to a rich society

to clear one's throat	sich räuspern
plump	pummelig
kettle	Wasserkocher
⚡ **chile** *US Dialekt*	Kind
to sort sth. out	etw. regeln
⚡ **hollerin'**	Brüllen

lady from Atlanta? A lady who has just died right before her eyes? She can't think of any relationship that makes sense. Where is he if Ms. Harrington was his contact? She obviously knew her father well and trusted him. He must have trusted her just as much. Why else would Ms. Harrington know why he is in Atlanta? He didn't even tell his own daughter. What if her father is in trouble? Something very odd is going on here. First, the disappearance and the mysterious envelope; now, the ring.

Penelope realizes that her best option is to go along to the police station with everyone else and see how much information she can get from others.

Another thought hits her, and she can feel her heart pounding. Maybe her father is staying here at the mansion. Wouldn't Ms. Harrington have offered Penelope's father that, too, if he is an old friend of hers? But… if he is staying here – why didn't he turn up last night? Didn't Ms. Harrington tell Penelope's father that she was coming?

Exercise 11: Word order. Bringen Sie die Wörter in die richtige Reihenfolge!

1. | heart | she | pounding | can | feel | her |

_____

2. | could | wish | my | I | father | find | I |

_____

3. | her | coffee | hands | she | Penelope |

_____

4. | knew | well | him | she |

_____

"Miss?" A policeman from the Atlanta Police Department has been shown into the kitchen by the maid. "May I ask you some questions?"

"Yes. Certainly, Officer."

The officer is studying her closely. He clears his throat and asks her, "Where were you last night, when Mrs…. Ms. Harrington died?"

"I… uhm… actually, I was holding her when she died," answers Penelope.

She can feel a **horrific** sensation[i] cours-ing through her body when she remem-bers yesterday's events.

"I see," answers the police officer, writing that down. "Can you accompany us down to the **precinct** now and give us your **statement**?"

False Friends	
sensation ≠ Sensation	
sensation	Wahrneh-mung, Ge-fühl, Empfin-dung
to cause a sensation	Aufsehen erregen

"Of course," says Penelope. "Could you just give me a moment to get my handbag? I'll be right with you."

Shehe looks at the cook and realizes that this is probably the only chance she has to ask if her father is staying here at the mansion.

"Excuse me," she says, handing the cook her half-full cup of coffee. "Is there anyone else staying here at the house?"

"Why yes, chile," the cook replies. "There is one other gentleman stay-ing here. But Jennifer, the maid, knocked on his door this morning, and it seems he hasn't woken up yet. He's been here for I think about four or five days now. He's a very charming gentleman. You know, the European-style charming."

maid	Hausange-stellte
horrific	entsetzlich
precinct	Polizeiwache
statement	*hier*: Zeugen-aussage
to dash sb.'s hopes	jds. Hoffnun-gen zunichte-machen

Penelope feels her heart pound in excitement. Maybe this gentleman is her father? The time frame definitely fits. Her father has been missing for about five days now. And he is one hundred percent European-style charming.

But **her hopes are dashed** in that same second, because Penelope hears the cook addressing the officer.

"Would you be wanting Mr. Dempsey at the precinct for questioning, too?" she asks.

It isn't my father after all, realizes Penelope.

"Yup. Him, too," answers the policeman. "Please tell him that he should come down to the station ASAP. I'll send another police car by, and all the staff should come for questioning too, okay?"

Penelope goes upstairs to her room to get her handbag. Lying right next to her bag on the dresser, she sees the ring and slips it in her pocket. It doesn't seem wise to leave it here.

Exercise 12: True or false? Kreuzen Sie die korrekten Aussagen an!

1. Penelope doesn't finish her coffee. ☐

2. Penelope finally finds her father. ☐

3. Mr. Dempsey has to go to the precinct for questioning. ☐

4. Penelope doesn't have to go to the precinct now. ☐

5. Penelope hides the ring in her room. ☐

Thirty minutes later at the police station, Penelope is asked to give her name and current address to the officer at the front desk. She gives them Ms. Harrington's address. Another policeman leads her into one of the interrogation rooms. It's just like the ones that she has seen a million times in American movies.

"Someone will be with you in just a few minutes," says the policeman before he closes the door.

Penelope is left sitting alone in the room. She hears the clock over the door ticking loudly. Everything that has happened in the last few hours seems so unreal to her. Was it only yesterday morning that she went looking for her father in the hothouse? Unbelievable! She can feel the **strain** of the past 24 hours and rubs her eyes. They are burning with exhaustion. Four hours of sleep simply are not enough. The jetlag has set in. She pulls her chair up closer to the desk, folds her hands, and presses her folded hands to her forehead. Penelope's thoughts are interrupted by someone opening the door. Turning around, she sees a police officer walking toward her, who looks completely **worn-out**. It's obvious that he's had a long night, too.

ASAP (as soon as possible)	schnellstmöglich
dresser	Kommode
current	*hier*: aktuell
interrogation room	Verhörraum
strain	Belastung, Strapazen
worn-out	erschöpft
drawl	gedehnte Sprechweise, hörbarer Akzent
sb. can't help but...	jmd. muss einfach ...
rugged	markant, rau

"Have a seat, ma'am," he says.

His Southern **drawl** is also quite strong. But from him, it sounds just charming, thinks Penelope. He must be at least 6.2 feet tall. His eyes are wonderfully green and gentle and are a lovely contrast to his darkish skin. He's obviously got the best of many different cultures. In a way, he reminds her of Keanu Reeves.

She takes his hand and, just like that, it seems a perfect fit. Penelope relaxes into his handshake and **can't help but** stare at him. He has a **rugged** style about him that keeps him from being too handsome. He is wearing a T-shirt, jeans and a holster. There is no gun in it.

In den USA wird das angloamerikanische Maß-system verwendet, das keinen Bezug zum Dezimalsystem hat:
1 inch (Zoll) = 2,54 cm
1 foot (Fuß) = 30,48 cm
1 yard (Schritt) = 0,91 m
1 mile (Meile) = 1,6 km
6.2 feet entsprechen also 189 cm.

Another officer enters the room, but he is obviously only there to take her statement of the incident. He nods to Penelope and leans against the wall. He could be the first policeman's twin – in blond.

Exercise 13: Pronouns. Ersetzen Sie die hervorge-hobenen Wörter durch Pronomen und schreiben Sie die Sätze neu!

1. **Penelope** is left sitting alone in the room.

   _____

2. **Penelope's** thoughts are interrupted.

   _____

3. **The policeman** reminds Penelope of Keanu Reeves.

   _____

4. Penelope folds **her hands.**

   _____

5. **The policeman's eyes** are wonderfully green.

   _____

This must be his partner, Penelope thinks. I'm sure he won't be saying much. He's so good looking, too – cops really are different to Bobbies. Penelope glances back to the first policeman. It's a nice sort of 'different,' she decides. This is a man I would definitely like to get to know better under other circumstances.

He is looking her over in much the same way.

"You must be Mrs. Penelope Battersea," the first policeman says.

"Miss not Mrs.," answers Penelope.

"And please call me Penelope."

"And I am Daniel. Detective Daniel Fitzgerald," he replies with a **twinkle** in his eye. "I'm the **investigating** detective in this case. You can call me Daniel. This is my partner, Detective Nathan Montgomery." He points to the other officer.

Penelope tries to keep her voice calm when she asks, "So this is a case? A real investigation case? I don't understand. Why? I mean… not really, is it? Why? Because ob-

incident	Vorfall, Ereignis
⚡ bobby *UK*	(Streifen-)Polizist
with a twinkle in one's eye	mit einem Augenzwinkern
investigating	ermittelnd
reflection	*hier*: Nachdenken
suspicious	verdächtig
unconsciously	unbewusst
mutual attraction	gegenseitige Anziehung

viously Ms. Harrington has died, but why is there an investigation?"

"Well, ma'am. The sudden or unexplained death of an individual usually leads to a police investigation in America."

Daniel pauses for **reflection**. "Investigating is what a detective like me does when two people who are working together die under **suspicious** circumstances."

With her eyes wide open in shock, Penelope asks, "Two people? Which two people?"

"Actually, I'm the detective here," says Daniel with a smile. "So I should be asking the questions. This probably all seems a little strange to you. You're not from here?" he says charmingly.

Is he flirting with me? Penelope wonders.

"Actually, no, I'm not. I'm from London," she answers and **unconsciously** leans in closer to him.

A few seconds go by in which they both feel the chemistry building up between them. The atmosphere in the room becomes more and more intense with their **mutual attraction**.

Exercise 14: Translation quiz. Übersetzen Sie und enträtseln Sie das Lösungswort!

1. Dame   __ __ □ __
2. Polizeiwache __ __ □ __ __ __ __
3. Nachdenken   __ __ __ __ __ __ □ __ __
4. Zeuge   __ __ __ __ □ __ __
5. Bulle   □ __ __ __
6. Frage   __ __ __ □ __ __ __
7. unterschiedlich __ □ __ __ __ __ __ __
8. unglaublich   __ __ __ __ __ __ □ __ __ __
9. sanft   __ □ __ __ __

Lösung: __ __ __ __ __ __ __

The other detective leans forward, and then Daniel clears his throat, breaking the mood.

Daniel continues in a more detective-like voice. "Yes, as I was saying, there have been two deaths. Ms. Harrington died last night. And two days before, at another Junior League event, her personal assistant died, too. The **medical examiner** tells me that they both didn't die of natural causes. So what we have here is an open criminal case that reaches into the Junior League of Atlanta society."

Two deaths? Not natural causes? And Penelope was holding one of the **victims** when she died? This is just too much.

Penelope usually spends her days peacefully assessing paintings and researching artists for the art gallery where she works. What has she gotten herself into? Or better, what has her father gotten her into? Maybe now she should tell Daniel about the ring and all.

But Daniel continues before she has made up her mind. "I guess Junior League doesn't mean much to you?"

Penelope shakes her head.

"Well, basically," Daniel carries on, "it's just a group of well-to-do ladies of Atlanta's jet-set with a lot of time on their hands. I'm not saying that their projects and fund-raising are not good. It's like the ultimate Atlanta jet-set competition."

"You obviously don't like them very much," Penelope replies.

"No, don't get me wrong. They do a lot of good things. It's just not always for the right reasons. Anyway, what I really meant to say is that two days ago, the Junior League had another event. Ms. Harrington organized this fund-raiser for child abuse victims with the BABG – that's the British American Business Group. They are a group of top investors and British business people who work here."

medical examiner	Gerichtsmediziner
victim	Opfer
to assess	schätzen, beurteilen
well-to-do	gut situiert
child abuse	Kindesmisshandlung
tax agent	Steuerbeamter
HMRC (Her Majesty's Revenue and Customs)	britische Steuerbehörde
far-fetched	weit hergeholt

"I see," says Penelope, not seeing at all. "So Ms. Harrington was well connected to British business people here in Atlanta?"

Maybe that's the connection, she thinks. After all, her father is a tax agent for the HMRC. Maybe he was investigating a British businessman who wasn't paying his taxes?

It seems a bit far-fetched, but it's the first explanation for her father's disappearance that makes any sense at all. But if so, why hadn't her father told her he was going to the US?

Exercise 15: Verb forms. Lesen Sie weiter und setzen Sie die korrekte Verbform ein!

"Anyway, two days ago there **1. be** _____ this event," Daniel continues. "Ms. Harrington's personal assistant didn't **2. show** _____ up. His name **3. be** _____ Josh Duvane. So Ms. Harrington **4. ask** _____ a Mr. Dempsey, a visiting friend of hers from England, to search for him. Mr. Dempsey went to Ms. Harrington's mansion and **5. find** _____ Mr. Duvane. He called the cops and an ambulance when he realized that Mr. Duvane was no longer **6. breathe** _____."

Daniel takes a deep breath and gives Penelope an intense look. Then he adds, "But you know all that already, right?"

"Why would I know that?" she asks. This is really confusing.

"Well, because you are also a houseguest of Ms. Harrington's. Aren't you also staying in the big house on Valley Road in Buckhead?"

"Yes, I suppose I am," answers Penelope.

She wants to add something, but is interrupted by Daniel waving his arm. He is pointing outside the office at an elderly gentleman coming toward them.

Daniel opens the door, steps outside and walks toward the gentleman. Penelope can't see the man's face properly because he has his hat pulled low over his eyes. He is wearing a trench coat and something about him makes her stare. Daniel is standing in front of her, blocking the gentleman from Penelope's view.

"Aah, Mr. Dempsey," she can hear him say. "We were just talking about you."

Daniel steps aside and Penelope can't believe her eyes. Her heart floods with relief. Everything will be fine now that she has finally found her father.

She is just about to rush forward and hug him when she detects something like wariness in his

to suppose	annehmen, vermuten
elderly	ältere(r)
properly	vernünftig
relief	Erleichterung
to detect	entdecken, wahrnehmen
wariness	Wachsamkeit, Vorsicht

eyes. Then her father holds out his hand in a formal gesture.

"Charmed, I'm sure," he says.

Shocked into silence, Penelope shakes hands with her father. What is going on?

Exercise 16: Definitions. Ordnen Sie den Wörtern die passende Definition zu!

1. ☐ silence   a) a large amount

2. ☐ relief   b) stop or hinder from speaking

3. ☐ flood   c) condition of being comfortable

4. ☐ believe   d) absence of sound

5. ☐ interrupt   e) accept as true

3 A HOODED STRANGER

Penelope throws her father a questioning glimpse. Why is he **pretending** that they don't know each other? He is her father, a tax inspector from London.

That's what she always thought, anyway. Now, she doesn't know what to think. Who is this man who simply disappears, leaving her no clue of his **whereabouts**? And then he turns up again in the middle of a police investigation in America?!

However, her father refuses to make eye contact and turns away, talking to Daniel. As usual, he

to pretend	vortäuschen
whereabouts *pl*	Aufenthaltsort
softly	*hier:* ruhig, leise
on the other hand…	andererseits …

speaks **softly**. When her father uses this tone, it makes everyone around him feel as if they are the most important person in the world. It makes her father seem taller and more powerful than he really is.

He hands Daniel a list. "I did what you asked me to do, Detective Fitzgerald. This is the list of people who were at the fund-raiser of the BABG on the day Mr. Duvane died."

"Thanks so much, Mr. Dempsey," says Daniel. "I'm sure this will help the investigation."

What is going on? Why is her father working with the police? Penelope is more confused than ever.

She clears her throat and tries to think of a way she can join in the conversation. Maybe now is the right time to tell Daniel and her father about the ring.

On the other hand, maybe the ring will get her father into trouble! She needs to speak to him alone first.

Exercise 17: True or false? Kreuzen Sie die korrekten Aussagen an!

1. Penelope is happy to see her father. ❒

2. Penelope knows why her father is acting the way he is. ❒

3. Daniel is meeting Mr. Dempsey for the first time. ❒

4. Penelope's father has a charming way with people. ❒

But it is Daniel who turns to her, not her father.

"Penelope, I need to talk to Mr. Dempsey about some details concerning Ms. Harrington. Would you mind getting yourself a cup of coffee in the hall? I'll be with you in just a second."

Penelope is too scared to say anything, so she nods and turns away from the two men. Before she can take a step into the hallway, however, she feels a hand holding her back.

"Miss Battersea," says her father to her. "I think you dropped this." He hands her a folded note.

"I… erm… well…," stutters Penelope. She doesn't remember dropping anything.

"No, really, this must be yours. I just saw it fall out of your handbag, when you came to the door," he says once more.

Too confused to speak, she takes the note with a nod and makes her way to the **vending machine**.

Maybe a cup of coffee is exactly what I need, she thinks. How I wish I had a cigarette with me. It's been three years since I quit smoking, and I'm still thinking about cigarettes.

Shaking her head at herself, she turns the corner and sees the vending machine in the hallway. In the movies, these things never work. The good-looking actors always lose their money and kick the machine.

Glancing around for someone who can help her, she decides to **give** the machine **a go**. Penelope checks her jeans pocket for change and pulls out three ten pence pieces.

Oh no, she thinks. I don't have any American money. Now what?

Exercise 18: Match up the phrases. Welche der folgenden Satzteile gehören zusammen? Ordnen Sie zu!

1. ☐ This is exactly	a) I quit smoking.
2. ☐ It's been three years since	b) what?
3. ☐ Would you mind	c) what I need.
4. ☐ Now	d) getting yourself a cup of coffee?

Penelope leans against the wall and closes her eyes. This is all a little too much for her. The good-looking detective, her undercover father, two dead people, and now no coffee.

A sudden thought re-energizes her – the note. Quickly, she unfolds it. In her father's handwriting, she reads:

Meet me at the Hard Rock Café on Peach Street, opposite Peachtree Centre at 6 this evening. Will explain all. Bring the detective.

At six this evening? Penelope's thoughts are interrupted by Daniel who has suddenly appeared beside her. **Peering** past him, she can see her father walking toward the exit. He gives her and Daniel a friendly wave.

"How very charming Mr. Dempsey is," Daniel says. "So British. You know, Penelope, we Americans have quite a few **prejudices** when it comes to you English. But I think that comes from us not really knowing any English people. I myself haven't yet met an unfriendly British person."

vending ma-chine	Getränkeau-tomat
to give sth. a go	etw. (mal) pro-bieren
to peer	spähen, schauen
prejudice	Vorurteil
IRS (Internal Revenue Ser-vice)	US Steuerbe-hörde

Penelope really doesn't know what to say to Daniel's comment, so she decides to change the subject altogether.

"You've known Mr. Dempsey for a long time then?"

"Not him personally," says Daniel. "But I've worked with some of his colleagues before."

"His colleagues?" asks Penelope nervously. "What does Mr. Dempsey do? Is he a police officer?"

She feels the blood rushing to her cheeks. As always when she gets nervous, Penelope starts playing with her hair.

"Not exactly," Daniel explains. "Some of his British colleagues have worked with the **IRS** before. We coordinate their missions from the police station."

Missions? What missions? thinks Penelope, running her fingers through her hair.

Exercise 19: Contracted forms. Schreiben Sie die Sätze mit Hilfe von Kurzformen auf!

1. "I do not have any American money."

   _____

2. "I myself have not met an unfriendly British person."

   _____

3. "You have known Mr. Dempsey for a long time then?"

   _____

4. This will not help the investigation.

   _____

"I'm a little surprised that you don't know that," says Daniel, smiling. "Just like I am surprised that it seems you two haven't met before. You're both staying at Ms. Harrington's mansion, after all. I mean, I know it's a really big house! But it's not *that* big!" He smiles at her. Is he flirting with me? Penelope thinks again. It looks like it. But there is something else **lingering** in his voice, too. Something careful.

She makes a decision to trust Daniel. At the same time, she knows she can't tell him everything before she has spoken to her father. So she needs to change the subject, and the only way she can think of is to flirt with him, too.

"Yes," she says with a twinkle in her eye. "That might sound a little odd at first, but I'll tell you all about if you buy me a cup of coffee."

Daniel hesitates. Then he smiles a lovely smile that makes her **go** a little **weak in the knees**.

"I won't buy you a coffee here, Penelope. It's just awful. But how about I buy you dinner?"

"Uhhmm… erm… ahem…"

"Here's my number," says Daniel. He hands her his card and scribbles his cell phone number on the back.

"I have a meeting with the Chief in two minutes. So I can't take down your statement myself. But my partner Nathan will do that for me," he continues.

Daniel calls out to his partner,

to linger	*hier*: nachklingen
to go weak in the knees	weiche Knie bekommen
to wink	zwinkern
witness	Zeuge
standard procedure	übliches Vorgehen
cubicle	Box in einem Großraumbüro
to text	*hier*: SMS schreiben
to spot	sehen, erkennen

"Hey Nate! Can you take over for me here with Ms. Battersea from London?" he asks, turning to her and **winking**. "Just take down her **witness** account and make sure she gets a ride home, okay?"

Turning back to Penelope, he says, "I'll pick you up at eight, okay?" Nathan gives Daniel an odd look. This is obviously not **standard procedure**.

Penelope nods to Daniel and follows Nathan down the hall to a **cubicle**. How much craziness can happen in just one morning?

Around six o'clock that day, Penelope is sitting in Ms. Harrington's limousine. She has **texted** Daniel that he should meet her at the Hard Rock Café at quarter past six. She hopes he'll come. And she is making sure to be there just a few minutes earlier so she can have a moment alone with her father.

Turning onto Peachtree Street, she **spots** the Hard Rock Café. It is just opposite an enormous, fancy-looking office building. She asks

Bartholomew to slow down. Maybe she can see through the window if her father is already there. Normally, this is not something she would do, but somehow the rules have changed. Everything has changed. Penelope is scared about what she might find out.

Exercise 20: Match up the characteristics. Ordnen Sie jedem Charakter drei Eigenschaften zu!

1. Penelope: ☐☐☐   2. Daniel: ☐☐☐

a) beautiful

b) rugged

c) good-looking

d) worries a lot

e) runs fingers through hair

f) gentle eyes

But Hard Rock Cafés all over the world are a tourist magnet. This one is no different. There is no way she can see through the windows. The view is blocked by a Japanese group of tourists entering the Café. Two backpackers in sandals are discussing something in front of another window. As Bartholomew passes the Café, Penelope looks out of the limousine's sunroof instead.

The Americans really know about **high-rises**, she thinks. What a difference this is to London. London might be pulsating with creativity and in some ways it is still **cutting-edge**, but in other ways London seems so idyllic compared to a mega city such as Atlanta.

Everything here is so extremely big. The streets, the houses, even the milk cartons at the supermarket are huge.

Penelope asks Bartholomew to drop her off two streets **down** from where she is meeting her father. Maybe some fresh air will help sort her thoughts.

She is worried about telling Daniel that she lied to him earlier on. Her father will surely tell him the truth now. Why else would he want to meet her and 'explain all' and ask her to bring Daniel along?

Bartholomew pulls the limousine up to the **curb**. "Are you sure you want me to drop you off here?" he asks in a skeptically.

Penelope doesn't really **register** what he is saying. Her thoughts are too tied up. She just nods at Bartholomew and he drives off.

high-rise	Hochhaus
cutting-edge	supermodern
down	*hier*: entfernt von
curb	Bordstein
to register	*hier*: merken
metropolitan	großstädtisch
to stumble	stolpern

Vorsicht
Verwechslungsgefahr!
to desert verlassen
[dɪ'zɜrt]
desert Wüste
['dezərt]
dessert Nachtisch
[dɪ'zɜrt]

When she peers down the road, she realizes that this is a completely different neighborhood altogether. Peach Tree Center further up the road has a **metropolitan** air to it. All the business people make it very urban. This huge building at the end of the road is enormous and very high-tech, too. However, there is no one here. This street is deserted [i]!

Shrugging, Penelope's thoughts turn back to Daniel. There probably won't be a dinner date. Daniel will think she is a liar and then…

Suddenly, Penelope **stumbles** and almost falls down, but catches herself just before she does.

Exercise 21: Odd one out. Welches Wort ist das „schwarze Schaf"? Unterstreichen Sie!

1. smile · nod · look · happy

2. plane · limousine · mansion · police car

3. pretending · confused · truth · questioning

4. completely · surely · disappearance · always

5. pulsating · idyllic · cutting-edge · metropolitan

"What the…?" she shouts after the man who nearly ran her down. "Excuse me, you nearly…!"

The man turns around for a moment. Penelope **squints** automatically and looks directly at him. Something about this man seems familiar. He is carrying an expensive-looking bag made of crocodile leather on his shoulder.

to squint	blinzeln
to freeze	*hier*: erstarren (lassen)
gaze	Blick
sidewalk *US*	Bürgersteig

Has she seen this bag before? Then Penelope realizes that the man is staring past her. And the expression in his face is one she has only noticed in movies – pure fear.

She feels goose bumps on her skin. The look of sheer terror in a grown man's face is not something you come across very often. It twists all of his features, **freezing** them into a sort of mask. This is horrible. What is this man so afraid of?

She turns her head, following the man's **gaze**. And then, thump. She is knocked over again. This time her hands hit the **sidewalk**.

She looks down and realizes that she has scrapes on both her hands.

She gets up – mad. This is really quite enough, Penelope thinks.

"Hey!" she shouts. "You could really apologize. I mean…!"

But her voice is lost to the person who has passed her.

The way the figure is walking is so spooky that Penelope closes her mouth. He passed her as if she were not there. He is so close that she can nearly hear him breathe. The hood of his grey sweatshirt covers his face. His clothes are quite baggy, but Penelope still notices that this man is slim. He is also not very tall. Penelope can tell by his movements that he is very athletic, just like her.

scrape	Schramme, Kratzer
spooky	unheimlich
hood	Kapuze
predator	Raubtier
to head toward	auf etw. zusteuern
hoodie	Kapuzenpullover
to make out	*hier*: erkennen, ausmachen

But there is something else about him. Yes, that's it – this person is not *walking* behind someone else. This person is *hunting* the man with the crocodile bag. He is like a dangerous predator – walking nearly silently.

Instinctively, Penelope follows the two men. She has no idea why. The hunter and the crocodile bag man turn up the road and head toward the Hard Rock Café.

The man with the hoodie gets faster with every step. Penelope starts walking faster, too, and her steps get louder. The hooded figure hears her footsteps and turns around. Penelope stops abruptly. Has she now become the hunted?

The only thing Penelope can see inside the hood is a dark blue bandana. The person is wearing a cap inside the hood, and Penelope can't even make out any eyes.

She is chilled to the bone.

Exercise 22: Unscramble. Lesen Sie weiter und bilden Sie sinnvolle Wörter aus dem Buchstabenchaos!

A car **honks**. Penelope's and the hooded figure's ___1. yese___

_____ are **distracted** for just a second. And

this moment is ___2. gehonu___ _____.

The hooded ___3. grufie___ _____ seems to

remember something. He turns around and ___4. skrabe___

_____ into a run, following his **prey**.

He reaches into his sweater, and Penelope notices that he

has on ___5. lovseg___ _____. She catches

a glimpse of the object. The man **flicks** it, and she

___6. zeferes___ _____.

It's a knife.

Oh God, this is serious. She must do something!

Speeding up, Penelope sees the **revolving door** of the Hard Rock Café just up ahead. The man with the crocodile bag is less than three steps away from the door.

"Get out of the way!" he shouts at the tourists ahead.

They turn around and quickly move to the side. The man in the hoodie has almost caught up with his victim now. The first man is about to reach for the door. But just as he tries to enter, the door starts revolving.

A second later, another man is standing outside on the sidewalk. He seems to be searching for something.

"Father," screams Penelope when she sees who the man is. "Careful! He's got a knife!"

Penelope's father turns around when he hears her voice.

"Pen…!" he shouts.

But his cry is halted when the two men bump into him with full force. Penelope's father is thrown off-balance and crashes into the glass of the still revolving doors.

For a second everything around Penelope seems to grow ice cold. She sees her father collapsing. Blood

to honk	hupen
distracted	abgelenkt
prey	Beute
to flick	*hier*: auf-schnappen lassen
revolving door	Drehtür
to gush	*hier*: hervor-strömen
in disgust	entrüstet

gushes from his head where it hit the door. Her father is not moving. She takes a step toward him and bends down.

"No!" she screams. "Father, wake up!"

Penelope hears another scream right next to her. It's the other man; the one who was being followed. He is lying just a foot away.

Oh God, she knows this man. It's the guy from the fund-raiser – the man who hugged Ms. Harrington!

Exercise 23: Verb forms. Lesen Sie weiter und unterstreichen Sie die korrekte Verbform!

The hooded man is **1.** sit / sitting on top of him and is

2. holding / holds the knife above his head. Penelope

3. is watched / watches **in disgust**. The screaming

victim is desperately 4. struggles / struggling and trying to protect himself. But he can't get his attacker off of him.

Penelope sees the knife 5. to come / come down in a swift movement.

Frozen stiff, Penelope is close enough to hear the knife cutting through the victim's clothes. The man with the bag makes a loud grunting noise and tries to get away from the knife. He seems much stronger than the hooded figure. This is his chance – the man being chased reaches up to grab the knife. But the hunter pushes his knee into his victim's face. The man with the bag falls backward in pain. He groans and his arms move instinctively to his face. The hunter shifts position and aims for the neck.

swift	schnell, flink
to grab	ergreifen
to shift position	die Position verändern
heart-piercing	markerschütternd
to stab	(zu)stechen
carotid artery	Halsschlagader
to spurt	spritzen

Penelope cannot believe she is witnessing something so horrible. She holds her breath and looks on in complete surprise.

The knife comes down, and Penelope knows that she will never forget the scream that follows. It is heart-piercing. She watches helplessly as the hooded figure stabs the knife into his victim's carotid artery in a swift movement.

Silently, the killer twists the knife. It seems to Penelope as if the whole world goes red. Blood is spurting everywhere.

Exercise 24: Crossword puzzle. Lösen Sie das Kreuzworträtsel!

Across

1. the boss of the detectives

4. another name for policeman (*slang*)

5. U.S. name for an investigating police officer

7. If you don't have a direct flight, you have a...

Down

2. a sweatshirt with a hood

3. What detectives do when they are looking for a criminal.

5. If you are not alive, you are...

6. to kill somebody on purpose

After just a few seconds, the victim's screams die down and his movements become slower. All that is left are gurgling sounds, which rock Penelope **to the core**.

Then, just as quickly as it happened, the attacker pulls out the knife and hides it in his pocket. He runs away around the next corner at full speed.

to the core	bis ins Mark
penetrating	eindringlich
to trickle	tropfen

Deeply shocked, Penelope kneels on the sidewalk. Around her, people are shouting. From the corner of her eye, she sees someone running toward them from down the street. It's Daniel.

He is yelling something to her. But Penelope can't hear anything. She is staring at the man lying on the ground. He has turned his head, and the look in his eyes is **penetrating**.

It is the fear of death.

Daniel gets to the wounded man and tries to stop the blood loss, but the man continues to lose blood.

Penelope glances down at her father. Blood is **trickling** through his grey hair from a wound on the back of his head. His eyes are closed, and he is not moving.

Penelope's world goes black.

4 WHEN THE MUSIC PLAYS

Penelope is sitting in the waiting area of a hospital. She is holding a glass of water that a nurse gave her. **Absently**, she notices the blood **stains** on her jeans. Her ponytail holder has come loose, her hair is a **tangled** mess, and her hands are trembling.

Now she remembers how she **fainted** at the Café. An ambulance had brought her to the emergency room a few minutes ago. When she had woken up in the ambulance, the friendly **paramedic** had spoken to her in a gentle voice. Penelope had asked about her father, and the paramedic had told her that he was unconscious and had been taken to the same hospital.

absently	geistesabwesend
stain	Fleck
tangled	verheddert
to faint	ohnmächtig werden
paramedic	Sanitäter
wound up	*hier*: aufgedreht
ward	Station im Krankenhaus

Since then, Penelope has been sitting here and no one has told her anything about her father. Across the room she sees Daniel talking to a group of doctors. But she is too **wound up** to wait around for him.

She walks to the reception desk, and the nurse tells her to go up to the neurological **ward** on the second floor. When Penelope takes the elevator up, her thoughts go back to everything that happened.

She can't believe what is going on, that she had just seen someone being stabbed. All that blood…

The man who was stabbed is the guy I met just before Ms. Harrington died. And Father is pretending to be Mr. Dempsey. And he lived at Ms. Harrington's place. What has Father gotten himself into? And what has he gotten *me* into? What about that note? I need some answers. Oh God, I hope he's okay. Please, God, let him be okay!

Penelope's worry and anger are all mixed up, and she is breathing heavily.

Why couldn't he just tell me what he is up to? Why the weird note? What was this guy from the party doing at the Hard Rock Café at the same time I was supposed to meet Father? Was this planned?

Exercise 25: Match up the opposites. Ordnen Sie den Wörtern die passenden Gegenteile zu!

1. ☐ trembling   a) conscious

2. ☐ kind   b) doubt

3. ☐ unconscious   c) hurtful

4. ☐ gentle   d) steady

5. ☐ believe   e) intense

Penelope gets out of the elevator. "Excuse me. I'm looking for a gentleman who came in with an ambulance. There was a stabbing at the Hard Rock Café," she says to a nurse.

"Ah, yes. I'm sorry. You can't see him right now," answers the nurse. "The doctors said 'no visitors' until he wakes up."

"So he's still unconscious?"

"Yes, I'm afraid so," the nurse replies.

"I see… I will…"

Before Penelope can finish her sentence, Daniel is standing by her side.

"I'll take over from here," he says to the nurse. "Come with me, Penelope. How are you feeling?"

He places his hand on her lower back and gently guides her to a row of chairs in the hall.

"I'm okay," she answers quietly. "I'd just like to know what is going on."

"Hmm," he answers, deep in thought. "I'd like to know what's

to monitor	überwachen
concussion	Gehirnerschütterung
stitch	Stich
agitated	aufgebracht
puzzled	verwundert

going on, too. But you've had quite a scare. Let's just sit down a moment, okay?"

"No, I want to know how my… my… I mean… how Mr. Dempsey is." Her voice has taken on a shrill tone.

"Yes, of course. Mr. Dempsey," Daniel tries to calm her down. "You'll be happy to hear that Mr. Dempsey is fine. The doctor just told me that they'll be monitoring him all through the night. At the moment he's sleeping. It seems as if he only has a slight concussion. The wound on his head needed three stitches…"

"He needed to be stitched up?" cries Penelope in an agitated voice.

Daniel's eyes widen, puzzled. "You seem very worried about him." He pauses a moment as if to analyze all the events of the last few hours in his head.

"Yes," he continues quietly. "Mr. Dempsey did get a few stitches, but the doctor told me that the cut wasn't so deep. All he needs is some rest, and then he'll be as good as new."

They look at each other in silence for a moment. In both their minds, they are replaying the horrific scene in front of the Café.

Exercise 26: Fill in the verbs. Lesen Sie weiter und ergänzen Sie die fehlenden Verben!

| meet | know | break | surprised | look |

Daniel is the first to **1.** ▒▒▒▒▒▒ the silence. He

sounds **pensive**. "I was really **2.** ▒▒▒▒▒▒ to see Mr.

Dempsey there. I mean what a **coincidence**. You ask me to

3. ▒▒▒▒▒▒ you there, and he shows up as well..."

Penelope **4.** ▒▒▒▒▒▒ at him and decides that she

doesn't **5.** ▒▒▒▒▒▒ what to say.

Penelope doesn't want to lie to Daniel. So she takes a deep breath and says in a quiet voice, "The other man. The one who was stabbed by... you know..."

"Yes...," says Daniel **reassuringly**. "I know. That must have been awful for you."

He kneels down in front of her. "My partner Nathan is on the **scene** at the moment. We are pretty sure that Ms. Harrington's death and this situation are connected. You were at the scene before I got there. So I'm afraid I need to ask you some more questions. But before that, there is something you need to know."

Daniel takes her hand and looks into Penelope's eyes. "The man who was stabbed... he died while you were unconscious. There was nothing we could do."

"But...," stutters Penelope.

"No, Penelope, there was nothing you could do."

"I know. It's just that… well, I… I don't know how to say this… but I think I knew him."

Daniel raises an eyebrow. "You knew Mr. Berger?"

"Berger. That's right. I couldn't remember his name earlier. I met him at the GACC function."

"I see."

"No, you don't see!" Penelope feels as if she is losing control. "He was killed right before my eyes. Yesterday a woman died in my arms, and I don't know what is going on! My own father…"

"Penelope," Daniel tells her in a strong voice. "You need to calm

pensive	nachdenklich
coincidence	Zufall
reassuringly	beruhigend
scene	*hier*: Tatort
to regain one's composure	seine Fassung wiedergewinnen
apologetic	entschuldigend

down. You've been through a lot and it's late. I think it's best if I take you to the police station. Then you can go home and get some rest. Tomorrow we'll…"

"No!" Penelope raises her voice.

A few nurses turn and look at her. She tries to **regain her composure** and takes three deep breaths.

"I mean, I can't face going to the house now. *And* I can't go to the police station. Really, I can't. It's just that…"

"You're right, Penelope," Daniel replies. His tone is **apologetic**. "What a fool I am. Of course you don't want to be alone in that big house after what you've been through. We can go to the police station later. But you know what? I guess I will take you to dinner after all."

"I don't think dinner is something I can deal with right now," she says.

"Fine. But we do need to get out of here for a while."

Daniel gets up and holds out his hand to her. "I know just the place. Trust me."

As they walk toward his car, Daniel's phone rings.

"Oh, hey, Nate. Hold on. What? No, I'm not at the station. Yes, she is here with me."

He pauses and listens. "No, I can't come now. You'll have to fill in the Chief by yourself. I know… Yes, I realize that the Chief is under a lot of pressure from the Mayor's Office. They'll get answers tomorrow."

Daniel nods at Nathan's answer, trying to keep calm.

"Yeah, I know you're under a lot of pressure, too. Listen, I am still here at the hospital. Why don't you…"

He is interrupted again.

to fill sb. in	jmd. informieren
irritated	ärgerlich
to cover for sb.	*hier*: jds. Arbeit übernehmen
relieved	erleichtert
to tremble	zittern
to steer	steuern, lenken
quaint	idyllisch
engulfed	umringt

"Okay. Fine. Let me know. No, don't worry. No, I know *exactly* what I'm doing…" Now, Daniel sounds a little irritated.

"Nathan… yes, I'll bring her in for questioning later. Yes!"

Daniel hangs up just as they reach his car. Penelope realizes that what Daniel is doing with her might get him into trouble. She is a key witness to a crime. And she's watched enough movies to know that they should both be going to the police station and not for a drive.

Exercise 27: Adjective or adverb? Lesen Sie weiter und unterstreichen Sie die richtige Variante!

"Don't you have to go to the police station and speak to the Chief?" she asks **1.** quietly / quiet . "Maybe I should go there first. I mean…"

Daniel shakes his head **2.** forceful / forcefully . "Nathan is **covering for me**. He's the chief investigator at the Café scene. I'll be there for the **3.** importantly / important press conference tomorrow, and you can give your statement then. Don't worry, it's all under control."

He puts on some **4.** softly / soft rhythm & blues music. For the next thirty minutes they just drive and enjoy the music. Penelope is **relieved** that Daniel is giving her a few moments to herself. At the same time she is **5.** extremely happy / extreme happily to be in his company. She looks down at her hands which are folded in her lap. They are **trembling**.

Daniel **steers** his car out of downtown Atlanta to the Virginia Highlands. The further they go, the less everything seems like a mega city. Something about the **quaint** neighborhood has a calming effect on Penelope. Daniel turns onto North Highland Avenue and parks the car. Getting out, they are immediately **engulfed** by the crowd of university students from Georgia Tech who seem to have all come out for the night.

Penelope relaxes when she sees and hears music all around her. It's coming out of the jazz and rhythm & blues bars, as well as from the musicians who are playing on the sidewalk.

This is the real South, she thinks and **soaks up** this easy-going, Southern joie de vivre. Daniel takes hold of her hand.

Just before they go into a club called 'Mama's **Joint**,' Penelope looks behind them. Earlier, she thought a car might be following them. She still has that feeling right now. This hooded figure has really scared her. But she can't detect anything suspicious, and she knows that she is safe with Daniel. He's a police officer, after all.

Exercise 28: True or false? Kreuzen Sie die richtigen Aussagen an!

1. Daniel returns to the police station after he met ☐
   Penelope at the hospital.

2. Penelope calms down when they are leaving ☐
   downtown Atlanta.

3. Penelope thinks someone is following her. ☐

4. Daniel's partner is worried. ☐

From the outside it looks like an old cabin. Penelope notices that the place is full; cigarette smoke **lingers** heavily in the air. Black and white posters of rhythm & blues stars from the 'good ol' days' are hanging on all the walls. The band is **tuning** their instruments. Daniel and Penelope have to squeeze through a lot of people until they reach the bar.

A young lovely African-American woman with a big smile walks

to soak up	aufsaugen
joint	*hier*: Schuppen, Spelunke
to linger	*hier*: hängen, verbleiben
to tune	stimmen (ein Instrument)

toward Daniel. She is tall and has the same wonderful eyes that Daniel has. Only her **complexion** is a lot darker.

"Danny-boy!" she shouts happily. "How are you, sugar? You looking for a quiet table for yourself and your **ladyfriend**?"

Daniel nods and gives her a hug. "Yeah. Penelope, meet my sister. Clarissa, this is my friend Penelope."

Clarissa waves them through. They sit down at a French-style bistro table at the very back of the room, right next to the back door.

"This way you two **lovebirds** can listen to the music and also hear yourselves speak. Two **cranberry fizzes**?"

Daniel nods and his sister winks at him. "Comin' right up."

Daniel points to the stage. "Now you've met my kid sister. Over there on the stage is my dad. He's the drummer. And the lady with the long red dress holding the **mike**? That's my mom."

complexion	Teint
ladyfriend	weibliche Bekannte
lovebirds *pl*	Turteltauben
cranberry fizz	Longdrink mit Cranberrysaft
⚡ **mike**	Mikro
civil servant	öffentlicher Angestellte
sip	Schluck

"Wow! That's quite a family," answers Penelope.

"Yeah, well. In real life, dad's a lawyer and momma works as a **civil servant**. Anyway, music is their passion."

The band starts playing their first song. Clarissa brings them their drinks and smiles at Penelope.

Hmm, she thinks, taking her first **sip**. What a lovely drink.

Penelope and Daniel enjoy the first few songs in silence. Then he glances at her and asks her if she is feeling better.

"Yes, I'm fine. Thanks so much for taking me here. This is lovely."

"I'm happy you like it," says Daniel smiling slightly. "I wonder, dear Penelope. How long will you be staying in Atlanta?"

"Why are you asking?"

"Well, to tell you the truth, I was hoping to get to know you a bit better once this investigation is over…"

"I see," says Penelope, blushing.

She doesn't answer him, but clears her throat.

"Concerning the investigation. Can I ask you some questions?" she asks instead.

"Fine," Daniel replies hesitantly. "What do you want to know?"

Exercise 29: Compound nouns. Bilden Sie zusammengesetzte Begriffe!

1. ☐ love   a) investigator
2. ☐ police   b) conference
3. ☐ chief   c) bird
4. ☐ press   d) student
5. ☐ university   e) station

"Well, for starters, I'd like to know if you think there is a connection between Ms. Harrington's death, the death of her assistant and the attack on Mr. Berger," asks Penelope.

"That's a very good question. Nathan just told me on the phone that Pete – that's the pathologist – is checking something out. It looks as if Ms. Harrington and Mr. Duvane died of multiple organ failure. Mr. Duvane was in his mid-twenties, and Ms. Harrington was in her late fifties, so he cannot say for sure at this point that there is a connection."

"Are you saying they both just fell over and died?" asks Penelope. How perplexing.

"Something like that. Except that Pete texted me earlier when we were still at the hospital saying that apparently Mr. Duvane had some sort of a **liver condition**. Right now everything is unclear. The first thing tomorrow, we'll have to start investigating the events of the past few days more closely. With the help of Mr. Dempsey's list, we're going to start questioning everyone who knew Ms. Harrington."

"I see."

Penelope is speechless for a moment, wondering what to do. She wants information from him, but she doesn't know how to **go about** getting it without sounding too curious.

hesitantly	zögerlich
organ failure	Organversagen
liver condition	Leberkrankheit
to go about sth.	etw. angehen
suspect	Verdächtige
incredible	unglaublich

Daniel interrupts her thoughts. "I'll begin questioning Ms. Harrington's Junior League friends tomorrow. The first lady on my list is a Mrs. Carmine."

"I remember Mrs. Carmine from the party last night," exclaims Penelope.

Daniel gives her a questioning look. "Maybe you want to come along with me?"

Penelope is surprised that he is asking her this. Does he only want to spend time with me or does he think I'm a **suspect**?

"Of course, I will," she answers. Her fingers are playing with her hair nervously.

Daniel nods and seems pleased with her answer. "I realize that this must all seem **incredible** to you. I mean, Nathan told me you only landed in the US yesterday, right?"

She nods.

"And then you went straight to the GACC fund-raiser where you met Ms. Harrington. Did you see Mr. Dempsey there, too?"

"Well, actually, yes and no," says Penelope. She doesn't answer the last part of the question. "I met Ms. Harrington there and some of her friends. One was Mr. Berger and the other was her lawyer. I can't remember his name."

Penelope pauses, trying to shake off the images of Mr. Berger's **gruesome** death.

Daniel says, "Mr. Berger. Poor man. I mean nobody deserves that kind of death. Not even him."

"What do you mean?"

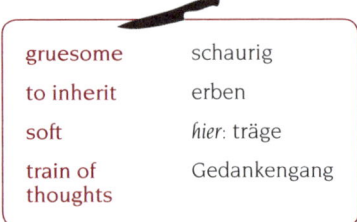

gruesome	schaurig
to inherit	erben
soft	*hier*: träge
train of thoughts	Gedankengang

"Well, he did have quite a reputation in Atlanta, our Mr. Berger. He used to go by the name of…"

"The Voice!" Penelope interrupts Daniel. "Now I remember. That's what he said to me last night. He said, 'My friends call me Tommy The Voice Berger.'"

"Ah, yes," says Daniel. "About fifteen years ago, 'The Voice' was something like the 'great white hope in blues music.' He was young. I don't think he was even eighteen when he landed a number one bluegrass hit in the charts. He was heading for a great international career, but then there was some sort of a scandal. I can't remember. I suppose all the media attention went to Berger's head. He got mixed up with the wrong kind of people."

"You mean drugs and stuff?"

"Well, more like sex, drugs and rock 'n' roll. Except soon, there was only too much of the first two and no more[i] music. But I think that's what sometimes happens to these Junior League people. They don't have to work for their money, they just **inherit** it. It makes them…"

Achtung! **no more** hat verschiedene Bedeutungen:	
no more…	kein(e) … mehr
no more… than	nicht mehr … als
… no more	nicht länger

Exercise 30: Negation. Verneinen Sie die folgenden Sätze!

1. Pete texted me that Mr. Duvane had a liver condition.

_____

2. Daniel interrupts her thoughts.

_____

3. I remember Mrs. Carmine from the party last night.

_____

4. You went straight to the GACC fund-raiser.

_____

5. I remember!

_____

"Soft. Yes, I can just imagine. I suppose that can happen in the best of families," Penelope agrees.

"And the best of families is definitely where young Tommy came from," adds Daniel cynically. "Did you know he was Ms. Harrington's nephew?"

Penelope shakes her head. "No, I didn't. But they did seem extremely happy to see each other at the function last night. They were obviously close."

"And now they are both dead."

They sit in silence for a moment, each one following their own train of thoughts.

"But what was Mr. Berger doing at to the Hard Rock Café earlier?" Penelope asks. "Or wasn't he heading there at all? Maybe he was going somewhere else?"

"I have no idea. Maybe it's a coincidence. He was definitely followed there by the hooded guy. But I think this all has something to do with Mr. Dempsey. He is, after all, the missing link in this investigation."

Exercise 31: Missing nouns. Lesen Sie weiter und ergänzen Sie die fehlenden Substantive!

link   list   morning   party   police station

time

"What? The missing **1.**   ?" asks Penelope, bewildered.

"Yes, he was at the Hard Rock Café and he found Mr. Duvane. *And* he was at the **2.**   last night when Ms. Harrington died. He told me so this **3.**   when he gave me the **4.**   . Did you see him there?"

"Mr. Dempsey? No. I didn't. The first **5.**   I met him was at the **6.**   this morning."

Penelope feels terrible, lying to Daniel.

"So it's just another coincidence that he was at the Hard Rock Café, too? You didn't know he was going to be there?"

This is starting to feel like an interrogation.

"Yes, well…," Penelope stutters.

She decides that she will try and stick to the truth as closely as possible. "Actually, remember when he handed me a piece of paper that I had supposedly dropped?"

Daniel nods.

"Well, I hadn't dropped it. The note was from Mr. Dempsey."

missing link	fehlendes Bindeglied
bewildered	verwirrt, verblüfft
supposedly	angeblich
government	Regierung
What on earth …?	Was um Himmels willen …?

Penelope pulls out the piece of paper from her purse and gives it to Daniel. He reads it and looks at her in surprise.

"Aha. Now I'm totally confused. Why didn't Mr. Dempsey ask me to meet him directly? I thought he was working with us…?"

"I don't know," answers Penelope truthfully. "How was Mr. Dempsey working for you anyway?"

"Well, he wasn't really working for me. It's just that in cases like this we sometimes help the British government."

"The British government? What on earth do you mean?"

"Well, that's why he was in the States. Mr. Dempsey was looking for a British businessman who isn't paying his income taxes like he should be."

"Oh yes, that!"

Penelope holds her breath. What is she going to do? Now she finally knows why her father came to America in the first place. Still, this doesn't explain why he is calling himself Mr. Dempsey.

Penelope needs a moment by herself to gather her thoughts.

"Daniel," she asks, hoping her voice doesn't sound as worried as she feels. "Would you excuse me for just a second?"

1	2	3	4	5	6
20	21	22	23	24	7
19	32	33	34	25	8
18	31	36	35	26	9
17	30	29	28	27	10
16	15	14	13	12	11

1-10: the group of people that rules a country

10-14: The opposite of a lie is the...

14-17: to be optimistic that something will happen

17-24: another word for "lift"

24-32: plural of where you go to "powder your nose"

32-36: to look at somebody for a long time

"Certainly," he says getting up and pulling her chair out for her. Penelope heads through the crowd of people. They are everywhere, dancing, singing, talking as she tries to get to the restroom. When she is almost there, she sees something that makes her blood run cold. Standing in front of the restroom is the hooded figure. The killer turns his head and stares at her.

So she was right! Someone *had* followed them here. It's the same guy. All she can see are his eyes. They are ice-cold and blue. Penelope screams **frantically**.

frantically	verzweifelt, wie wild

5 NEW PERSPECTIVES

Penelope stands glued to the spot.

This man, the man who killed Mr. Berger, is going to kill me, too.

From the corner of her eye, she sees a movement. Then Daniel's body **hurtles** into hers with a painful **thud**. He pulls her down to the floor with him, away from the killer. They both crash into the surrounding tables.

Penelope's breath is knocked out of her as she hits the floor. Daniel is lying across her, protecting her with his body. Penelope's chest hurts, and her arm feels as if it is being ripped off. She lifts her head and looks up – right into the killer's eyes.

He doesn't blink. Penelope feels his **piercing** stare as if he is **literally** touching her. She is **terrified** and still can't move.

Daniel rolls off of her and turns over so he is facing the killer as well. The hooded man is just standing there. For a second, Penelope's and Daniel's eyes are locked on the killer.

He is so close. Penelope is scared to death.

to hurtle	sausen, schleudern
thud	dumpfer Schlag
piercing	stechend, durchdringend
literally	tatsächlich, wirklich
terrified	verängstigt
at the top of his voice	so laut er kann
ϟ to yank	ruckartig ziehen
fierce	*hier*: grimmig
to take sb. on	es mit jmd. aufnehmen

And only now does she realize what is hurting her arm. The killer is holding on to her purse with his right hand. Penelope holds on tight. Is that why he followed us? Is he looking for something that belongs to me? she desperately thinks.

The room has gone dead quiet. But Daniel has been trained for action when everyone else freezes. Lifting himself upright, he holds Penelope down on the ground and starts shouting at the top of his voice.

"Atlanta PD! Stay right where you are!"

At this, the hooded figure takes a step back and lets go of the bag. He quickly turns away and starts running toward the exit.

"Someone stop him!" Daniel hollers

He quickly looks around the room, assessing the situation while trying to get back on his feet.

One man reacts to Daniel's loud cry. The man holds out an arm and grabs the hoodie. The hooded figure is yanked backward and nearly falls over. Simultaneously, the hooded man pulls something out of his pocket.

It's a knife.

Everyone standing around him immediately takes a step back, and the man who was holding the hoodie lets go. The hooded figure turns around, holding up the knife. His eyes are fierce-looking as he focuses on the people standing closest to him; he challenges anyone to take him on.

Everyone is holding their breath while Daniel makes his way through the crowd as fast as he can.

"Police!" Daniel shouts again. "Stop!"

He pulls out his gun. "Everybody get down!"

Penelope slowly gets to her feet.

I hope Daniel knows what he's doing, she thinks.

"Stay right there," Daniel commands the hooded man in a quiet, controlled voice.

They are both standing only a few feet from the exit of the bar. The crowd starts closing in on the hooded figure. The **presence** of a police officer has given them new confidence.

"Danny!" screams a high voice from the stage.

Daniel's head **whips around** as he reacts to his mother's voice. That second is all the hooded figure needs. While everyone is looking toward the stage, he ducks and pushes his way out into the dark Atlanta night.

presence	Anwesenheit
to whip around	herumschnellen
to grunt	grummeln, grunzen
entire	gesamte(r,s)
to seep	*hier*: schwinden

Daniel's mother puts her hand on her mouth. She stares wide-eyed, frozen in shock – partly from fear for her son and partly from realizing that she has just given the hooded figure a way out. Daniel **grunts** in anger and rushes out after him.

In the street, Daniel looks right and left up the road. There are crowds of people walking by as if nothing has happened at all. The evening temperatures have set in, and almost every second person is wearing a hoodie. The person who attacked Penelope and killed Mr. Berger could be anywhere. He could be anyone.

Daniel drops his hand which is holding the gun and shakes his head in frustration. This is the second time that the killer has escaped him in one day.

With a sigh, he turns around and walks back into the bar.

Penelope is sitting on a chair, surrounded by Daniel's **entire** family. She is silent and her body is shaking badly while everyone else is talking.

"Penelope?"

When Daniel says her name, she gazes at him with fearful eyes.

"Listen, everyone. Get back. Give the lady some space, okay?" Daniel says in his policeman voice.

He turns around and looks at his sister. "Clarissa? Can you get her a drink? A real drink."

She nods and turns toward the bar.

Daniel kneels down in front of Penelope for the second time that day and takes her hands.

"This man," Penelope says in a shocked voice. "Oh God, Daniel! Why did he follow us here? What does he want from me…"

Her voice gets ^{**i**} quieter as she feels all the strength **seeping** out of her.

become oder get?	
to become	werden
to get	erhalten; werden; bringen

Beide Verben können auch synonym verwandt werden, wenn ein Adjektiv folgt:
to become/get faster
Aber: nur **become** verwenden, wenn ein Substantiv folgt:
to become a detective
Und nur **get** verwenden, um „bekommen" auszudrücken:
When do I get my burger?

"We'll get him, Penelope," Daniel answers calmly. "I promise you. Everything will be okay."

Exercise 34: Verb forms. Lesen Sie weiter und unterstreichen Sie die korrekte Verbform!

Two hours later, at around 11 p.m., Penelope **1.** is / are

back in her room in Ms. Harrington's mansion.

The past hour at the police station **2.** has taken /

has taked what little strength she had left completely out

of her. The fact that Mr. Berger's killer **3.** followed /

follows them to the bar had changed everything. Now

there **4.** is / is being a direct connection between Berger

and herself.

After she **5.** has calming / had calmed down in the bar,

Daniel had taken her to the police station **6.** to become /

to get her statement.

Penelope had answered question after question while Daniel's partner had taken down her statement about Mr. Berger's death and the
attack at the bar. She had described the hooded figure as accurately
as she could: blue eyes, moderate build, athletic figure, not tall. Oh
yes – and she had remembered that she thought Mr. Berger's killer
had small feet. For some reason, that detail had struck her. When
she had been lying on the floor of the bar, Penelope had noticed the
small feet again. So yes, she was pretty sure that the two hooded
figures were one and the same person.

At the station, Daniel had been cold and reserved toward her. Maybe because he had to act differently with his colleagues around? Penelope is not sure. Daniel had been so wonderful earlier at the bar. And she had been so sure of their attraction for one another.

Oh, she can't think straight anymore. She feels so drained. All she wants is some peace and quiet.

Exhausted, Penelope rests her head in her hands, but she can't relax. Her heart is pounding, adrenaline pumping through her veins. Earlier at the police station, she had managed to stay calm. But now, all by herself, her mind is in overdrive from all the confusion of the day.

Was the hooded person trying to kill her? Or was he only after her purse? What could he be interested in? Is all this really happening?

This morning I was so happy to see Father at the police station. And now he is in hospital, someone else has died, and I am being followed. On top of it all, there is Daniel…

I can't sleep now, Penelope thinks. And I need a drink.

She opens the bedroom door and looks around. The house is quiet. This silence sends shivers down Penelope's spine as she looks around on the landing, thinking of Ms. Harrington.

build	Statur
to strike sb. as...	jmd. ... erscheinen
to drain	*hier*: aufzehren
to be in overdrive	auf Hochtouren laufen
to send shivers down sb.'s spine	jmd. einen Schauer den Rücken runterlaufen lassen
landing	Treppenabsatz

Forget the drink. I need some answers. And the only way I am going to get any is to start looking for them myself.

Quietly, Penelope starts walking down the landing. She feels like a criminal and knows that she should leave this work up to the police.

But she just can't help herself. One of rooms must be her father's, and she is determined to finally get some answers.

She tries to open the first two doors, but they are locked. On her third try, however, she get's lucky. The door opens.

Exercise 35: Questions about the text. Beantworten Sie die Fragen zum Text in ganzen Sätzen!

1. Is Penelope sure that Mr. Berger's killer and the attacker at the bar are the same person?

   _____

2. Did Daniel want to take Penelope to the police station before the attack in the bar?

   _____

3. Why is Penelope's statement important after the attack in the bar?

   _____

4. How does it make Penelope feel that someone was following her?

   _____

5. Is Penelope sure about Daniel's feelings for her?

   _____

As soon as she enters, Penelope knows she is in her father's room. It has the Battersea smell. Penelope smiles to herself. The Battersea smell is a mixture of her father's cologne, **potting soil**, and old books. At least that is what her school friends have always told her. Penelope closes the door behind her quietly. She finds the light switch to her left and **flicks** it **on**. Next to the bed, there is her father's messy suitcase. That's how he has always been: messy with his things, organized with his thoughts.

She glances at a pile of books on the desk in the center of the room. It's spooky to be looking through her father's things in a stranger's house in the middle of the night, but she must find out what is going on. Is her father really only investigating a **tax evader**?

Penelope **pulls up** the chair that is next to the desk and sits down. Looking over the papers and books, she notices her father's favorite pen and a list of names. No, there are actually two lists. One has the **head-**

potting soil	Blumenerde
to flick on	anknipsen
tax evader	Steuerhinter-zieher
to pull up	*hier*: heranzie-hen
heading	Überschrift
highlighted	hervorgeho-ben
to latch on	hängenbleiben an

ing GACC, and the other one has the heading *BABG*. Penelope sees about twenty names on the GACC list. She recognizes a few of them. Some of them are underlined, and some of them are **highlighted**.

Mr. Duvane's name is highlighted in green, Mr. McGraw in yellow. Mr. Berger's name is yellow, too. A number of other names are marked with a blue pen. Mrs. Carmine, Mrs. Potter, Mrs. Shaughnessy… are these all Junior Leaguers?

Penelope doesn't know what to make of this. Is this the list she saw her father give Daniel this morning at the police station?

Her eyes **latch on** to a yellow post-it sticking out of one of the books that are piled on the table. She pulls the book out; it's a UCLA yearbook from 1975. Penelope opens it on the marked page and looks at the faces of the young graduates of the class of '75. Her eyes stop at a picture of her father as a young man.

Exercise 36: Plurals and possessives. Bilden Sie die richtige Pluralform in Verbindung mit der Genitivform!

1. the room's light switch _____

2. her father's list _____

3. her father's favorite pen _____

4. the bedroom door _____

5. the graduate's face _____

That must be the day he got his ring, she thinks. The one he always wears on his right **index finger**. Why did Ms. Harrington have that ring? And why did she give it to me?

Scanning the page once more, she sees a picture of Ms. Harrington's in her twenties, smiling at the camera. So her father and Ms Harrington **graduated** together. They have known each other since college.

So maybe the ring was Ms. Har-

index finger	Zeigefinger
to graduate	einen aka-demischen Abschluss erwerben
horticultural	Gartenbau…
will	*hier*: Testament
beneficiary	Begünstigter

rington's? Every member of a graduation class gets one after all. Maybe her father really is only in Atlanta on tax business and visiting an old friend? But this still doesn't explain why he pretended not to know his own daughter.

She decides to keep looking. Going through the yearbook again, something else catches her eye – her father and Ms. Harrington were president and vice-president of the UCLA Horticultural Society. Therefore, Ms. Harrington shared her father's love of plants and gardening.

Penelope pulls out a paper that is half-hidden under the pile of books and starts reading. Her hands start to tremble when she realizes that she is holding a will – Ms. Harrington's will. And it names Mr. Thomas Berger as Ms. Harrington's main beneficiary.

That makes sense, Penelope thinks. After all, he is her nephew. Penelope swallows hard, or rather, he *was* her nephew.

There is also a post-it on the will. In her father's handwriting, Penelope discovers the word *d. cap*. What can that mean?

And what on earth is her father doing with Ms. Harrington's will? Penelope puts it down, and at the same time another paper drops onto the floor. It must have been stuck to the back of the will.

Penelope picks it up. It is a note which is made up of individual letters that are cut out of magazines or newspapers.

It reads:

> **TOMMY CANNOT INHERIT.**
> **YOU KNOW WHY.**
> **CHANGE IT.**

Oh god, it is a blackmailing letter. Did Father write this letter to Ms. Harrington? Penelope asks herself. Was he blackmailing her to change her will? Or is this from somebody else, and Ms. Harrington gave it to Father before she died? Maybe he was trying to find out who sent it? Is this message the reason why he is pretending to be Mr. Dempsey?

Penelope shakes her head. That can't be it. Ms. Harrington had known him for so many years.

Why did I **cover for him** when he called himself Dempsey and not Battersea? she realizes in a panic. Maybe he has done something horrible. Oh God! This is terrible. I can't believe I'm thinking such things about Father…

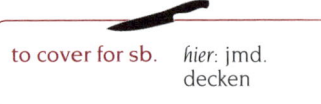

| to cover for sb. | *hier:* jmd. decken |

Exercise 37: Translation. Übersetzen Sie die folgenden Sätze!

1. They have known each other since college.

   _____

2. He wears the ring on his right index finger.

   _____

3. He pretended not to know his daughter.

   _____

4. The paper is half-hidden under the pile of books.

   _____

5. It is a note made up of individual letters.

   _____

6. Maybe he has done something horrible.

   _____

Alone in his office at the police station, Daniel is looking through the evening's reports. He has sent his partner Nathan home to his wife and newborn baby.

Daniel himself is too wound up to **call it a day**. He shouldn't have **taken** Penelope **into his confidence** today at the bar. It was wrong to give her all that inside information about an ongoing investigation. Nathan was right. That was really unprofessional behavior. Daniel realizes that his feelings for Penelope have **clouded his judgment**. She is a witness after all. And after the attack at the bar, she is also a **target**. He should focus on the facts of the case and not allow himself to get distracted by beautiful Penelope.

Okay, so Mr. Duvane worked for Ms. Harrington, and Mr. Berger was her nephew. And they are all dead...

Daniel hears his door open and looks up. In walks the **coroner** with an exhausted look on his face. From his **horn-rimmed glasses** to his odd choice of shoes and his messy haircut, Pete looks a hundred percent like a scientist. Like an elderly, **nutty** professor. Nonetheless, he is very good at his job. "Hey, Pete," Daniel greets him.

Pete nods. "Someone downstairs just told me you were back, so I decided to drop this off before I go home."

⚡ to call it a day	(für heute) Schluss machen
to take sb. into your confidence	jmd. Vertrauen schenken
to cloud sb.'s judgement	jds. Urteil trüben
target	Ziel(scheibe)
coroner	Gerichtsmediziner
horn-rimmed glasses	Hornbrille
⚡ nutty	verrückt, spleenig
preliminary forensic report	vorläufiger rechtsmedizinischer Bericht

He puts two **preliminary forensic reports** on Daniel's desk – Mr. Berger's and Ms. Harrington's. Daniel opens up the first file and reads that Mr. Berger bled to death.

Exercise 38: Personal pronouns. Lesen Sie weiter und ergänzen Sie die Personalpronomen!

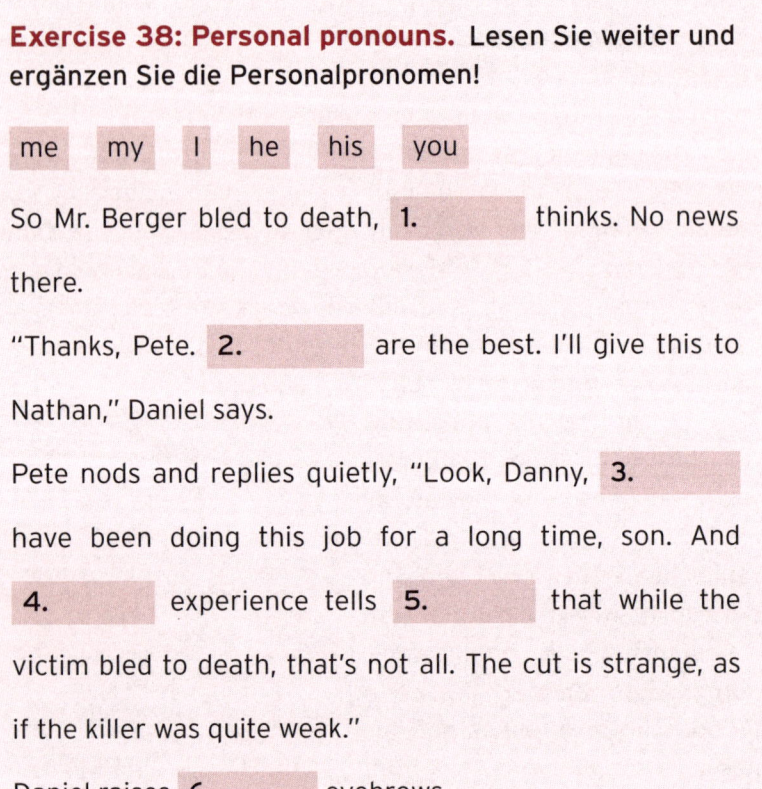

| me | my | I | he | his | you |

So Mr. Berger bled to death, **1.** ____ thinks. No news there.

"Thanks, Pete. **2.** ____ are the best. I'll give this to Nathan," Daniel says.

Pete nods and replies quietly, "Look, Danny, **3.** ____ have been doing this job for a long time, son. And **4.** ____ experience tells **5.** ____ that while the victim bled to death, that's not all. The cut is strange, as if the killer was quite weak."

Daniel raises **6.** ____ eyebrows.

"*And* I looked into the other report again. The one for Ms. Harrington's death. I compared it to her assistant's death. This Duvane guy had a liver condition. He must have had Hepatitis B or C at one time. And sometimes the liver never recovers from such a serious illness."

Pete looks at Daniel to see if he is listening closely. Then Pete continues. "That's why I think I there is a connection between Duvane's and Harrington's death: they both had **kidney** and liver **failure**. I'm thinking they **were poisoned**. Do you know why?"

Daniel shakes his head.

"Because that's what poison does. It destroys the organs one by one. In this case, it means: Duvane and Harrington could have been poisoned at the same time. But Duvane's liver condition would explain why he died before she did."

Daniel breathes in sharply.

That's it; that could be the proof of a direct link between Duvane's and Harrington's death, he thinks.

Daniel is about to start asking a question when Pete interrupts him.

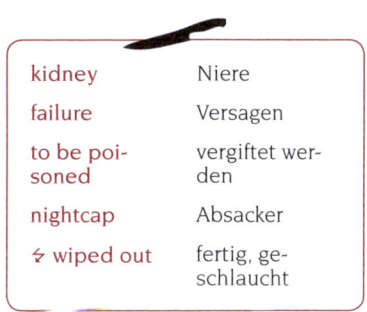

kidney	Niere
failure	Versagen
to be poisoned	vergiftet werden
nightcap	Absacker
⚡ wiped out	fertig, geschlaucht

"Listen, son, I've had a long day. I just want to get home to Jenny and a nightcap. I will make sure to get right on the analysis first thing tomorrow morning. I'm not sure what kind of poison we're talking about here yet."

He gives Daniel a direct look. "Go home, son. You look wiped out. Grab some sleep."

Daniel nods tiredly and rubs the back of his neck. "Good night, Pete."

Poison, he thinks as he waves good-bye to Pete. What I need now is a motive and a suspect.

He looks through the papers again and notices the BABG list that Mr. Dempsey gave him this morning. Quickly, Daniel compares the names with the list of the Junior League members that he and Nathan will begin questioning tomorrow.

He notices that most of the names are on both lists. Nathan will be questioning the four people whose names start with A and B, and he will start with the letter C. C for Carmine. Another name that's on both lists is Mr. McGraw. Nathan has already arranged to meet the lawyer tomorrow afternoon.

Exercise 39: Adjectives and adverbs. Lesen Sie weiter und ergänzen Sie die fehlenden Adjektive und Adverben!

possibly   slight   strong   suddenly   tall   well

Daniel **1.** _____ remembers what Pete just said - the stabber was **2.** _____ not a **3.** _____ person. He also recalls that Penelope said that the hooded figure was of **4.** _____ athletic build and not **5.** _____. Maybe the hooded figure is not a man after all, but a woman?

Daniel's experience tells him that women and poison fit **6.** _____ – poison is a **modus operandi** known to be favored by women.

Maybe there is also a connection between the stabber and the poison that Pete was talking about? He shakes his head. No, that's too much of a coincidence. And why would the hooded killer go around poisoning people? But how else does Berger fit in?

Daniel's detective **persona** kicks in. It could be a woman, he thinks. All the people on the lists are women – except for McGraw. Pete will find out exactly which poison we are talking about tomorrow. But why would someone poison a society lady like Ms. Harrington and her assistant? What could be the motive?

Who better to ask than someone who knew Ms. Harrington well; someone who was close to her during her last days? Mr. Dempsey. Daniel looks at his watch. It's nearly midnight so there is no way he can go to the hospital and speak to him. That will have to wait until tomorrow; after he has been to interview Mrs. Carmine.

And since Penelope was so worried about Mr. Dempsey earlier, he'll take her along with him after they question Mrs. Carmine. Just thinking of Penelope makes him smile.

Daniel frowns, realizing that he must **keep** his feelings **in check**. He decides to head home and get

modus ope-randi	Vorgehens-weise
persona	Persönlichkeit, Identität
to keep sth. in check	etw. unter Kon-trolle halten
to flip through sth.	etw. (schnell) durchblättern

some sleep. Getting up from his desk, he trips over a cardboard box.

That's right, Daniel remembers. This is the box with Mr. Dempsey's personal things. The paramedics had given it to Nathan, who had brought the box with him from the Café.

There's a gentleman's leather bag in the box. Daniel sits down again and drops the contents onto his desk. A book falls out, a ring, and a set of keys. Putting the keys aside, Daniel takes a look at the ring. It's a UCLA class ring. So Mr. Dempsey studied in the US once upon a time.

That's interesting. This morning at the police station we talked about California, and I asked him if he had ever been there. And he said no. Either this isn't his ring or he is pretending not to be a graduate of the University of California.

Daniel turns over the book and reads the title. It's about horticulture. **Flipping through** the pages, he sees pictures of orchids, vegetables, flowers…

Mr. Dempsey is interested in plants *and* taxes, thinks Daniel.

He can't put his finger on it, but all of a sudden, something about Mr. Dempsey doesn't **add up** anymore. Dempsey, UCLA, plants, poison… What is Mr. Dempsey's connection? What is he missing?

⚡ to add up — einen Sinn ergeben

Exercise 40: Translation quiz. Übersetzen Sie und enträtseln Sie das Lösungswort!

1. Pflanzen   _ _ _ _ _ ☐

2. Gedanke   _ _ _ ☐ _ _ _

3. erstechen   ☐ _ _ _

4. Gift   ☐ _ _ _

5. Kripobeamter   _ _ _ _ _ _ ☐ _ _

6. Verdächtiger   _ _ _ _ _ ☐ _

7. Niere   _ ☐ _ _ _ _

8. Untersuchung   _ _ _ _ _ _ _ _ _ _ ☐ _

9. Verbindung   _ _ _ ☐ _ _ _ _ _

Lösung: _ _ _ _ _ _ _ _

6 NOT IN TIME

Penelope looks over at Daniel. His hands are gripping the steering wheel tightly. He hasn't even glanced over to her since she got into his car ten minutes ago. Yesterday at the police station, Daniel had promised to pick her up at nine and he'd been on time.

Penelope clears her throat and says, "I called the hospital just now. The head nurse wouldn't tell me how Mr. Dempsey is doing…"

"But," interrupts Daniel, "after the ward rounds at ten o'clock, we can visit him, right?"

She looks at him in surprise.

"I am a cop, Penelope. Mr. Dempsey is a witness to a crime my partner is investigating and is involved in a crime which I'm investigating. I called the hospital this morning, too, and we'll go and see your Mr. Dempsey right after I finish questioning Mrs. Carmine."

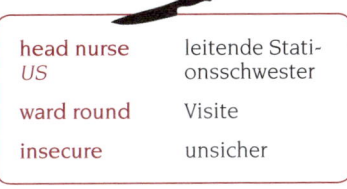

head nurse *US*	leitende Stationsschwester
ward round	Visite
insecure	unsicher

So that's what this is about, thinks Penelope. He has realized that he hasn't been acting like a professional when he took me to his parents' bar. That's why he is being so cold.

"Daniel, I really appreciate everything you've done. And I… it's just that…"

She doesn't know what to tell him, but hopes he will react to her. Right now, she is insecure about everything.

But Daniel doesn't answer. He turns on the radio instead.

Fine, thinks Penelope. I don't understand this man. And I'm not going to throw myself at him if he is acting like this.

She crosses her arms and looks out of the window. They cruise toward Highway 185 South in silence.

The farther they drive out of Atlanta, the more intrigued Penelope becomes by the vastness of the countryside. The high-rises and the metropolitan flair is gone. The five-lane expressway has signs that have mystical sounds to them: Chattanooga, Buford… this is the Deep South.

Daniel dials a number on his hands-free phone.

"Yup," says Nathan's voice after two dial tones. "Where are you?"

Exercise 41: Fill in the blanks. Lesen Sie weiter und ergänzen Sie die fehlenden Substantive!

answers   investigation   notes   voice   way

witness

"Nate, listen," Daniel replies. "I'm already on my

1. _____ to Mrs. Carmine's. That's my first

2. _____ this morning. I need you to check in

with the Chief before you go to your first one. You'll find my

3. _____ on my desk and everything else…"

Daniel is interrupted by Nathan, whose **4.** _____

sounds extremely irritated. "Now you want me to do the

press conference? What am I going to tell the Chief about your side of the **5.** _____ ? There'll be reporters wanting some real **6.** _____ . What's going on, Dan? This is not like you at all."

Nathan pauses and when he doesn't get an answer, he asks, "Are you alone?"

"Ms. Battersea is here with me," Daniel answers quietly.

"I see." Nathan's voice takes on a colder edge. "Okay, I'll get the press conference sorted out. Just get back here as soon as you can. We need to talk."

Nathan hangs up without a word of a good-bye.

Penelope **feels** very **awkward** at the way the conversation went. Embarrassed, she looks out of the window.

"Do you know a lot about plants?" Daniel's voice cuts through her thoughts.

"Well, yes. Erm, no. I mean, my father…," stutters Penelope, surprised at the question. "Why do you ask?"

"Well, the thing is, I **got a** new **lead** from the coroner yesterday. It's just a **hunch** and we don't have any **specifics** yet. But then I found

⚡ to cruise	_hier_: entspannt herumfahren
intrigued	fasziniert
vastness	unermessliche Weite
to feel awkward	sich unbehaglich fühlen
hunch	Ahnung, Gefühl
to get a lead	einen Hinweis bekommen
specifics _pl_	Einzelheiten

something in Mr. Dempsey's things that has made me think… Anyway, do you or don't you know a lot about plants?"

Penelope is not sure how to answer the question. She wants to stay close to the truth, because Daniel will know of her relationship to Mr. Dempsey once they visit him in the hospital.

Should she tell him the truth now? She bites the inside of her lip and runs her fingers through her hair.

"Look Daniel, there is something I have to tell you. I don't know how to put this. I…"

Daniel turns toward her. "Does this have anything to do with the investigation?"

Exercise 42: Correct the mistakes. Lesen Sie weiter und korrigieren Sie die sechs Fehler im folgenden Absatz!

"Well, yes," Penelope say's after a moment. "I would have told you earliest, but I was just so worried and confusedly. It's about something that happens on the nights Ms. Harrington died. Actually, it's two thing…"

1. _____ 2. _____

3. _____ 4. _____

5. _____ 6. _____

"Tell me," Daniel demands.

"Okay. It's like this. Just before Ms. Harrington died, she gave me something and…"

Daniel jerks his head around to scowl at her. "And you are telling me this now? Penelope, I'm giving you details of a case and you…"

His face has taken on a deep brown color, showing his anger.

"Daniel, please let me explain."

But Daniel doesn't say a word.

So Penelope continues, "She… she gave me a ring – she pressed it into my hand just before she collapsed."

"A ring? What type of ring?"

"A class ring from UCLA. It belongs to my father. I don't know why I didn't tell you. I was just worried that he might be mixed up in something terrible. You see, I came to Atlanta to look for him…"

"And your father knows Ms. Harrington?" Daniel asks quietly.

Another UCLA ring? he thinks. Does Mr. Dempsey know Penelope's dad? There are definitely too many loose ends here.

to jerk	(sich) ruckartig bewegen
to scowl	finster/mürrisch blicken
loose ends *pl*	offene Fragen
evidence	Beweis(e)
to curse	fluchen
⚡ shoot	Scheibenkleister
⚡ satnav	Navi
⚡ crap device	schrottiges Gerät

"Yes, I suppose… in a way…," says Penelope.

"In a way? How can you know someone 'in a way'?" Daniel's voice sounds extremely irritated now. "Penelope, Dempsey is somehow connected to three deaths. Harrington gives you a ring that you think belongs to your father, and your father knows Dempsey? This means that you have been holding back evidence in an ongoing police investigation. This is serious. I'll have to check this out once we get back to Atlanta."

He pauses. "Where is your father now?"

"Well, actually, that's the second thing I was going to tell you. My father…"

Penelope is interrupted by Daniel cursing. "Shoot! That's our exit. 278 East. Why doesn't this stupid satnav work? This is such a crap device…"

He hits the satnav with his fist. "Listen, Pen. Let's get Mrs. Carmine's questioning over with. Then we'll talk. You give me your father's ring when we get back and... aaah so this Covington."

Penelope looks out of her window. Covington is a quaint little Southern town, with a typical town square that displays the US flag right in front of city hall.

Daniel follows the satnav's directions to Mrs. Carmine's house.

Penelope doesn't know if she should be relieved or scared that Daniel is distracted at the moment. She decides to leave things as they are.

Exercise 43: Collocations. Wie lauten die Wendungen richtig? Ordnen Sie zu!

1. ☐ to jerk   **a)** something over with

2. ☐ to hold back   **b)** one's anger

3. ☐ to follow   **c)** ends

4. ☐ to get   **d)** one's head around

5. ☐ to have many loose   **e)** evidence

6. ☐ to show   **f)** directions

Ten minutes later, they drive over a bridge and through a lovely arch covered with roses. The road leads up to a charming old farm-house.

How beautiful it is here, thinks Penelope.

There is a red barn right next to the house. It looks as if it's the only thing that has been freshly painted in a long time.

I wonder if there are any animals here? she thinks, looking more closely. A reflection of some kind blinds her eyes, and she pulls her sunglasses out of her bag.

Before she can take a closer look, a pretty Caucasian woman comes toward the car from behind the barn. She must have heard the police car pull up. She is in outdoor clothing and wearing sunglasses.

"Welcome," she says to Penelope and Daniel. "Please excuse my outfit. I have just been outside gardening."

"Mrs. Carmine? My name is Detective Daniel Fitzgerald, and this is Ms. Battersea. I believe you two have met. We talked on the phone yesterday. I'd like to ask to you a few questions concerning the death of your friend, Ms. Harrington."

"Yes, certainly. I've been expecting you. Please come in."

Penelope and Daniel follow her

city hall	Rathaus
arch	*hier*: Brücken-bogen
engraving	*hier*: Stahlstich
davenport	Sekretär

into the house, and Mrs. Carmine excuses herself to wash her hands and get them some iced tea.

Penelope and Daniel look around the living and dining room area they are standing in. All the walls are decorated with old paintings and engravings of plants.

This woman must love all the different types of plants on the planet, Daniel thinks. What is it about plants in this whole case? There are pictures of flowers, vegetables, everything from roses to tomatoes and mushrooms.

Penelope goes a step closer. The drawings remind her of engravings that her father collects. Many of the Latin names she reads below the paintings are familiar to her.

Walking around toward the dining room, Penelope sees a picture of a young family on a davenport. There's a young pregnant woman, a little girl and a handsome man.

Exercise 44: Unscramble. Lesen Sie weiter und ordnen Sie die Buchstaben zu sinnvollen Wörtern!

"Please take a seat. Excuse me, if I leave my **1. gensussals**

_____ on." Penelope is taken aback by Mrs. Carmine's **2. cevio** _____. She feels like an **intruder**.

Mrs. Carmine continues, "It's just that I have been **3. girncy** _____ a lot since Judy's **4. hadet**

_____... I can't believe she's really gone..."

Mrs. Carmine hands them some iced tea in tall **5. slesgas**

_____.

Embarrassed at Mrs. Carmine's obvious emotional **distress**, Penelope changes the subject.

"Erm, yes… is this your family?" she asks and points to the photo.

"Yes," answers Mrs. Carmine in an unemotional voice **flatly**.

Daniel clears his throat and begins with his questions. He asks Mrs. Carmine to state her full name, date of birth, and for how long she has known Ms. Harrington.

"Judy and I have been friends for some years. I met her at one of these plant events that she sponsors."

Daniel continues, "Where exactly were you when she died?"

"Why, I was standing right next to… What's your name again?" Mrs. Carmine asks Penelope.

"Sorry. Penelope Battersea and…"

"Yes, now I remember. We were introduced that frightful night, just before Judy…"

Mrs. Carmine's voice grows quieter. She is obviously trying to keep herself from falling apart.

After she has regained control of her voice, she continues. "I was standing right next to Ms. Battersea when Judy collapsed. That's all I know."

"I see. How long had you been at the party?"

"About an hour, I would say."

"And where were you yesterday between 5 and 6 p.m.?"

"Well, let me think. I was here. Why are you asking?"

"I'm asking because this is when Mr. Berger was stabbed to death in downtown Atlanta."

"What? I… excuse me… I don't think…," Mrs. Carmine pauses and swallows hard. "What…? Mr. Berger was stabbed?"

"Yes, stabbed *to death*," Daniel re-plies. "Is there anyone who can confirm that you were here yesterday at that time?"

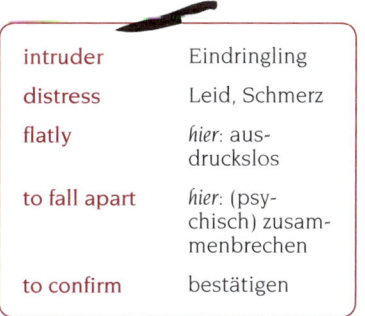

intruder	Eindringling
distress	Leid, Schmerz
flatly	*hier*: aus-druckslos
to fall apart	*hier*: (psy-chisch) zusam-menbrechen
to confirm	bestätigen

"I don't know… I was alone… I don't think…"

"Okay. I have one last question for you, Mrs. Carmine."

She looks at him.

"Where were you on the day Mr. Duvane died?"

Ten minutes later in the car, Penelope is still struggling with her anger. She can't believe how rude Daniel was to Mrs. Carmine. Mrs. Carmine had shown him an airline ticket to and from Los Angeles that proves that she was in L.A. on the day Mr. Duvane died.

1. "Where exactly were you when she died?" he asks.

   _____

2. "I can't believe she's really gone."

   _____

3. "Why are you asking?" she asks him.

   _____

4. "Excuse me, if I leave my sunglasses on," she says.

   _____

Why had Daniel been so unfriendly? Was it because he is angry with me? Does he really think that Mrs. Carmine is a suspect? Or does he have a problem with Mrs. Carmine, because she is a Junior League member?

"Look, Penelope," Daniel says, turning to her once they are back on the expressway. "I think it's best if you just give me that ring when we get to the station, okay? Do you have it with you?"

Penelope nods and her anger turns into a bad conscience. She realizes that Daniel has been quite patient with her, and she has been lying to him the whole time.

"Of course. I understand. And I'm sorry…"

She pauses. "Really, Daniel, I'm sorry. Of course I'll give you the ring. It's here in my purse. But please let's go to the hospital first, okay?"

Penelope is worried about her father and about Daniel's reaction when he finds out that her father is Mr. Dempsey.

"Give it to me when we get to the hospital, okay? And I still need to ask you some questions now. Police procedure."

"Okay."

"When exactly did you arrived in Atlanta?" Daniel asks.

"The day before yesterday. I flew Delta from Amsterdam and landed at about eight. Do you want to see my boarding pass? I'm sure I still have it here somewhere…"

"Listen, I'm only doing my job. You don't have to be so defensive," he says, his voice getting softer.

Exercise 46: Translation. Übersetzen Sie folgende Sätze!

1. Penelope ist sauer.

_____

2. Ich bin vorgestern in Atlanta gelandet.

_____

3. Er ist sehr geduldig mit ihr.

_____

4. Sie hat ein schlechtes Gewissen.

_____

5. Hör mal, ich mach' nur meine Arbeit.

_____

They pull up in front of the hospital, and Penelope grabs the door handle. But Daniel puts a hand on her left arm, motioning her to wait. His eyes search for hers. The moment feels strangely intimate. What does he want from me? thinks Penelope.

They both lean back.

Daniel's voice interrupts the silence. "The ring, Penelope?"

Oh. Embarrassed, Penelope takes it out of her bag and holds it up. Daniel shakes his head when he takes the ring from her. His left hand reaches into his car door. He pulls out a ziplock bag and puts the ring inside.

I am in so much trouble, he thinks. This ring is evidence which I should have had a day earlier, and now it's completely contaminated. Daniel pictures Nathan and the Chief shaking their heads at so much unprofessionalism.

to motion	bedeuten, winken
intimate	intim, vertraut
ziplock bag	wiederver-schließbarer Plastikbeutel
contaminated	verunreinigt

"Thanks," he says flatly. "I'll send it to forensics when we get back to the station."

Daniel moves to open the door. He is looking forward to questioning Mr. Dempsey, so he can get to the bottom of all this.

Just then, Daniel's phone rings. He stops moving and takes the call.

"Of course, Nate," he says. "No problem. I can make it in 15 minutes. I just got back from Covington. No. No problem."

Daniel listens to his partner for a moment longer and pulls up his eyebrows in surprise. "I see. Yeah. But why Lenox? Oh, okay. And is he bringing the documents?"

He hangs up and turns to Penelope. "I have to meet someone. When you've seen Mr. Dempsey, can you call me later? I have a few questions for him."

"What's going on?" asks Penelope.

"Some new information in the case. I'm meeting Mr. McGraw, the lawyer, at the Lenox Mall in fifteen minutes. He works just around the corner from the mall. Nathan can't make it."

Penelope nods her good-bye and gets out of the car. Her thoughts are all over the place. On the one hand, she is relieved that she now has the chance to talk to her father alone. On the other hand, she is curious about this meeting between Mr. McGraw and Daniel. Does this change of plan have something to do with Ms. Harrington's will?

Exercise 47: True or false? Kreuzen Sie die richtigen Aussagen an!

1. Daniel is looking forward to meeting the Chief and Nathan. ☐

2. Penelope is happy that Daniel is going to meet McGraw. ☐

3. Daniel can't go to Lenox Mall. ☐

4. Penelope doesn't want to visit her father. ☐

5. Nathan meets Daniel and Penelope at the hospital. ☐

Daniel switches on his blue lights and speeds through town. That's the only way he can make it to the Lenox Mall in fifteen minutes. When he gets closer to Lenox Square, he sees the main entrance of the mall. He heads into the parking lot. Nathan said that McGraw would be waiting near the East entrance. McGraw's law office is just around the corner from Lenox and McGraw doesn't have much time between two meetings. But McGraw urgently **insisted** that he needed to give Nathan something as soon as possible.

Driving in walking speed, Daniel takes a left turn.

That must be McGraw, thinks Daniel. The man is dressed in a conservative suit – typical lawyer **attire**. In his right hand, he is holding an envelope.

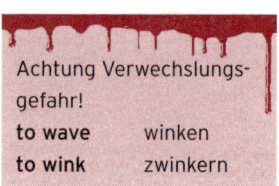

McGraw waves to Daniel when he notices the police car. Daniel pulls up the car, nods to Mr. McGraw, and indicates that he needs to find parking first. He circles the parking lot.

Daniel's head whips around suddenly when he hears **screeching tires**. In the **rearview mirror**, he sees a dark **convertible** come speeding around the corner. It is heading straight for McGraw.

Did someone follow me here? Maybe from the hospital? Daniel thinks.

He immediately hits the brakes and pulls the mouthpiece of the police radio toward him.

"This is Detective Daniel Fitzgerald. I'm at Lenox Mall and request backup. Now. There's a **rogue driver**. Driver might be armed. Over and out."

He needs backup right here and now. All at once, Daniel jumps out of the car and grabs his gun from his holster.

The oncoming convertible takes the same left corner Daniel took just a moment ago at **breakneck speed**. The tires of the automobile are smoking and screeching.

to insist	bestehen auf
attire	Kleidung, Aufzug
screeching tires *pl*	quietschende Reifen
rearview mirror	Rückspiegel
convertible	Cabrio
rogue driver	Amokfahrer
⚡ breakneck speed	Höllentempo
to run for cover	in Deckung gehen
toddler	Kleinkind

Achtung Verwechslungsgefahr!

to wave	winken
to wink	zwinkern

McGraw's face is gray, and his mouth is slightly open in fear when he sees the car hurtling toward him. He stands there absolutely frozen in shock.

Daniel runs toward McGraw while he is shouting at the top of his voice to surrounding pedestrians, "Everybody move! Run for cover!"

Exercise 48: Word search. Finden Sie die angegebenen Wörter!

rogue frantic unnatural breakneck hood

suit speed siren

W	T	S	Z	S	U	I	T	D	R
G	F	P	X	C	N	I	V	R	O
B	R	E	A	K	N	E	C	K	G
L	A	E	O	Y	A	T	Z	U	U
F	N	D	U	H	T	E	H	P	E
U	T	D	E	M	U	E	O	S	D
S	I	R	E	N	R	A	O	P	E
R	C	T	B	E	A	I	D	L	N
D	L	A	W	E	L	S	R	I	F

Two mothers passing in front of a nearby shop front are holding their toddlers by the hand. They pull their little children to their bodies quickly and break into a run. An elderly gentleman falls to

97

the ground. Two teenagers grab him under his arms and drag him out of the oncoming car's way. Everyone is screaming.

"Run!" shouts Daniel. "Run!"

He is about 2 yards away from Mr. McGraw.

"Move!" Daniel shouts at him. "McGraw, move!"

But the lawyer only stands there, not moving, and just looks at Daniel. It takes him a little too long to realize that he is this car's target. The driver **accelerates**.

A heartbeat later, there is a **sickening** thud as McGraw is hit. He flies through the air and lands on the **hood** of the car. For a horrific moment, his arms and legs are **flailing** about wildly. His body looks like a marionette. The car is still moving at full speed. McGraw is catapulted onto the roof. He rolls off and is thrown to the ground.

Then the car races past Daniel, and he catches a glimpse of a small figure in a hoodie. In a frantic, helpless move, Daniel **lunges** toward the car, but it is too fast. His eyes search for the license plate. However, the car is already turning the corner, and all he can

to accelerate	beschleunigen
sickening	entsetzlich
hood *US*	*hier*: Motor-haube
flailing	fuchtelnd
to lunge	einen Satz ma-chen
crumpled	*hier*: zer-quetscht
angle	Winkel

make out are the last two numbers: 72. Daniel hears police sirens. Oh, no! Not another death, he thinks.

Daniel turns around to McGraw. It's a horrific scene that meets his eyes: Mr. McGraw's **crumpled** body is lying motionless in a pool of his own blood. His arms and legs are bent at an unnatural **angle**. Someone will pay for this, Daniel thinks.

7 MIND OVER MATTER

Finally, Penelope is standing in front of her father's hospital room, feeling excited and scared at the same time. She takes a deep breath and enters.

Oh, God, he looks so old and frail, she thinks when she sees the bandages wrapped around his head and his pale face. I hope he is going to be okay.

Penelope puts a chair next to her father's bed, gently takes her father's hand and sits down. His eyes

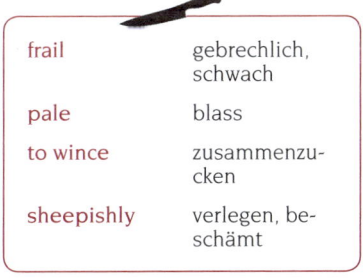

frail	gebrechlich, schwach
pale	blass
to wince	zusammenzu-cken
sheepishly	verlegen, be-schämt

flutter open, and it takes him a moment to focus. When he recognizes his daughter, his face breaks into a smile and he lifts his head. "Ouch," he winces in pain.

"Father," Penelope says softly. "Slowly. Don't worry. I'm here."

Her father sighs. There is a lot of emotion in that one sigh. For a moment, they just gaze at each other.

"Pen… I'm so happy to see you…"

Her father's voice breaks, and he swallows as if to keep his composure.

"Me, too, Father. How are you feeling?"

"I think, I'll be okay," Penelope's father says sheepishly. "I have to stay here until tomorrow."

He looks at her intently. "Pen, you need to tell me what's going on."

"Father, I don't even know where to start. This has all just been such a **nightmare**. I don't understand anything anymore. Ms. Harrington gave me your ring when she died. And I found that note on your desk in her house. Father, why are you here in Atlanta? Why are you pretending to be a Mr. Dempsey? Why did you pretend not to know me? I mean, you lied to the police… I can't cover for you anymore if you are involved in Ms. Harrington's death…"

Exercise 49: Word spiral. Finden Sie die Begriffe in der Wortspirale!

1	2	3	4	5	6
20	21	22	23	24	7
19	32	33	34	25	8
18	31	36	35	26	9
17	30	29	28	27	10
16	15	14	13	12	11

1-8: a place where you go when you are very sick

8-10: the truth is the opposite of a…

10-16: an adjective for feeling very emotional in a positive sense

16-23: Penelope is Mr. Battersea's…

23-31: to become aware of somebody's identity

31-36: Penelope finally… her father's hospital room.

"Pen!" Her father's voice sounds shocked. "How can you even think such a thing?"

"Listen, Father." Penelope's voice is harsh. "I've flown halfway across the world because I was worried sick about you. Nobody knew where you were! All I found in your hothouse was an address. Then I fly here, and someone dies in my arms. You pretend not to know me and…" She starts to cry.

"Oh, Pen. I'm so sorry. I never meant to hurt you. I've been such a fool."

Penelope wipes her eyes and looks at her father expectantly.

"Actually, I've been an *old* fool," he continues softly. "I'm afraid that Judy's death is my fault."

"What? Do you have something to do with her death?"

Penelope can't believe what she's hearing.

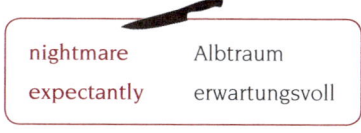

| nightmare | Albtraum |
| expectantly | erwartungsvoll |

"No!" Her father raises his voice slightly. He is very agitated. "I was just helping an old friend. You see, we went to university together and we've always kept in touch. Over the years, we've both enjoyed sharing information on horticulture."

"So you've been friends for years, and I never knew?"

"Well, Pen, even an old goat like me has his secrets," answers her father. "Anyway, all this time, Judy has been very helpful with her connections to the BABG. When our office has to look for British tax evaders in the US, someone from my department travels here under a false name so the tax evader doesn't know he is under investigation. Often, these business people show up at the Junior League BABG or GACC functions, because that's where business people network. Since Judy is so well connected, we can go to nearly any party."

"I see," says Penelope. "But what has that got to do with her death? Do you mean a British tax evader is murdering people? The person in the hoodie who killed Mr. Berger didn't look like a British businessman to me…"

Penelope's father interrupts her and asks quietly, "So Tommy died after the attack at the Café?"

"What, no one has told you?"

Penelope's father shakes his head. "Oh goodness, this is getting worse and worse. And it's all my fault. Nobody here told me anything. They said I should wait for the police. Where is Fitzgerald, by the way?"

"Daniel, erm, I mean Detective Fitzgerald is meeting the lawyer at the moment. I'm supposed to call him right after I've talked to you."

"What?"

"You heard me, Father," Penelope replies. "And what do you mean by 'It's all my fault'?"

"I only meant that I should have told the police everything right from the beginning," he sighs. "It's like this, Judy asked me to help her. She had been getting these letters…"

"I think I found one of them in the house…"

"I tried to find out who was behind it all, too. Judy didn't want to involve the police." Penelope's father clears his throat. "But then Josh died. And now Judy is dead, and Tommy was killed, too. What have I done?"

"Yes! What *have* you done? Tell me!" Penelope demands.

to be flattered	sich geschmeichelt fühlen
to blackmail	erpressen
⚡ to come clean	reinen Tisch machen

"I only wanted to help her. She suggested that I use my professional cover to investigate her private problem. I was flattered and tried to find out who was blackmailing her. I thought…"

He hesitates for a moment, but continues when he sees his daughter's skeptical look.

Exercise 50: To or too? Lesen Sie weiter und unterstreichen Sie die korrekte Variante!

"Well, I realize that was stupid," he adds. "And I shouldn't
have pretended not **1.** to / too know you. But that night
at the party, when Judy died, I was just coming over **2.** to /
too greet you. Then all of a sudden, Judy collapsed in your
arms, and I knew that things had gone **3.** to / too far.
I needed **4.** to / too check some things out before I **came
clean** with the police. Don't you see?"

"No, Father. I don't see," Penelope replies in a cold voice.

"I wanted to explain everything **5.** to / too you at the
Café," her father says. "I wanted to tell Detective Fitzgerald
everything, **6.** to / too . I just needed to speak to McGraw
first."

"Why?" Penelope is perplexed.
"Well, because McGraw told me on the GACC night that something
had come up that changed everything. He thought he knew who
was writing the blackmailing letters," he explains. He pauses and
looks his daughter in the eye. "And so I hoped that I could at least
solve the puzzle…"

"Father! What's wrong with you? This isn't a game! You are not a detective who can find criminals. You are sixty-two years old and a British tax officer!"

Penelope is losing her patience.

"I know…," her father says calmly.

"Father, I can't believe you made *me* lie to the police, too! I was protecting you. I thought you were in serious trouble. And all along I was only protecting your flattered ego?"

She turns away, and runs her fingers through her hair, thinking. Then, she turns back toward her father suddenly.

"So Ms. Harrington didn't have *your* ring? It was *her* ring?"

"Yes. We all got one at our graduation in 1975. I don't know why she gave it to you. But she knew I was going to talk to McGraw that night. We thought that maybe we had found out who was making the threats. I'm pretty sure that I'm on the right track with my hunch about d. cap."

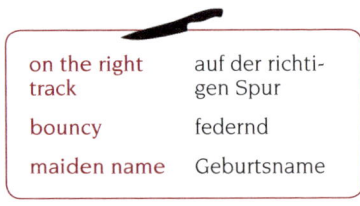

on the right track	auf der richtigen Spur
bouncy	federnd
maiden name	Geburtsname

"What? What do you mean?"

The hospital door opens, and a young nurse walks in with a bouncy step.

"Sir? I have to take you in for the scan now."

The nurse walks over to Penelope's father and helps him into the wheelchair.

"Maybe you can come back later, ma'am? This might take a while," she says to Penelope.

"Pen, when you see Detective Fitzgerald, tell him that it's Ms. Carmine and not *Mrs.* Carmine. Carmine is her maiden name," her father says, turning his head to her.

"What?"

But the nurse is already pushing him out of the room.

Exercise 51: Fill in the blanks. Lesen Sie weiter und fügen Sie die englischen Übersetzungen der folgenden Begriffe richtig ein!

| Tatort | Tode | Stunden | Spiegel |

| Sanitäter |

Daniel splashes water on his face and looks at himself in the

1. _____ . He looks exhausted. Drying off his face

with a paper towel, his mind runs through everything that

has happened in the last two 2. _____ .

The 3. _____ had taken McGraw to the hospital.

After securing the 4. _____ , the specialists had

taken over, and Daniel had gone back to the station. He had

just called the hospital, and they confirmed that there

was nothing they could do. McGraw is dead. Three

5. _____ in three days. Daniel sighs.

Walking to his desk, he sees both Nathan and the envelope that McGraw had been holding. Daniel had forgotten to give it to the forensic specialists on the scene.

"Hey, Nathan."

Daniel gives his partner a pat on his shoulder and then tells him everything that happened with McGraw.

After a moment of **stunned** silence, Nathan clears his throat. "Listen, Daniel, the Chief wants to speak to you, pronto. We'll talk later. I've got some news."

Nathan points to the Chief Inspector standing in the doorway of his office with a **stern** look on his face.

Chief Webber is a **bald**, very large African-American known for his no-nonsense leadership. Everything has to be done **by the book**. Typical ex-marine.

Daniel bites his bottom lip and takes a deep breath. He knows that he is in trouble.

"What do you have to say for yourself, Detective?" the Chief asks once Daniel has walked into his office.

"Chief, I …"

"No. Forget I asked that. I don't want to hear any excuses. I have the entire **town council** on my back, and I need some answers ASAP."

stunned	fassungslos, geschockt
stern	streng
bald	kahlköpfig
by the book	nach Vorschrift
town council	Stadtrat

Exercise 52: Adjectives. Ergänzen Sie die fehlenden Formen!

1. _____ _____ most exhausted

2. deep _____ _____

3. _____ sterner _____

4. stunned _____ _____

5. amazed _____ _____

Chief Webber pauses and continues in a quieter tone. "I understand we are looking for a man or a woman in a hoodie, who has stabbed one person and driven over another. And we are looking for someone who is poisoning people?"

"Yes, Chief... Please can I explain..."

"Listen, Detective. I respect your work. So I am going to give you 24 hours to get this mess sorted out and find us some **perps**. This morning's press conference is not something I wish to repeat. I need some real answers by tomorrow. And I don't want to hear anything else about you **fraternizing** with witnesses. Have I made myself clear?"

"Yes, sir." Daniel nods. "Crystal clear."

"Fine. Now get out of my sight!"

Nathan has been watching the entire scene from his desk. He gets up and gives his partner a **reassuring** pat on the back when Daniel comes out of the Chief's office.

With a **pained** smile Daniel says, "We need to find out who is behind all this. Here."

He hands Nathan the ring that Penelope gave him. "I need to get this to Pete as soon as possible."

"Fine, I'll take it down to him. But first, let me fill you in."

Daniel sees McGraw's envelope

⚡ perp	Täter
fraternizing	*hier*: unprofessionelle Nähe erlauben
reassuring	beruhigend
pained	gequält
Amanita phalloides	Grüner Knollenblätterpilz

still unopened on his desk and makes a mental note to open it once Nathan is done.

"Okay, so here's the thing," says Nathan. "Pete has run the blood tests, and one thing is for sure. Duvane, Harrington and Berger were all poisoned. It looks as if they all had the same dosage of... hold on... I can't remember the name of the poison... ah yes, here it is... it's from a mushroom called **Amanita phalloides**..."

"Poisoned by a mushroom? Who would have thought?" Daniel asks **incredulously**.

"Yeah, apparently this poison is pretty **vicious** because you don't feel the symptoms immediately, although it's deadly," Nathan explains to Daniel. "It takes you about five days to die. Pete said that a person who is poisoned in such a way would feel a little sick a day later and then forget about it. They would be having symptoms like **vomiting** and **diarrhea**. Basically like a stomach flu. Then, for like a day before they die, they feel a lot better. And on day five, bam, they die of multiple organ failure. Their heart fails, and they simply fall over and die. Like Ms. Harrington."

incredulously	ungläubig
vicious	heimtückisch, schrecklich
vomiting	Erbrechen
diarrhea	Durchfall
wreck	Wrack
lousy	mies
boozing	Saufen
to be quite the man	ein richtiger A-Promi sein

"I don't understand, they all died differently. It makes sense with Ms. Harrington. But where's the connection to Berger and Duvane? And McGraw?"

"Well, we'll see what's in McGraw's blood," Nathan replies. "But concerning Duvane, Pete said that because of his Hepatitis B or C, his liver was a **wreck**. And the first organ to go is the liver, then the kidney… etc."

"So what you're saying is that Harrington and Duvane could have both been poisoned on the same day?" asks Daniel. "And Duvane felt the effects more quickly and died sooner, because his liver had been destroyed by an earlier illness?"

Nathan nods. "Yeah, that's what Pete said. He is pretty sure that Harrington and Duvane were poisoned at the same time. They just reacted differently."

"What about Berger?" Daniel asks.

Exercise 53: Fill in the blanks. Lesen Sie weiter und ergänzen Sie die fehlenden Wörter!

poisoned	fitness	interesting	confirmed	scandal

"That's where it gets **1.** _____ . Berger was poisoned, too. But for some reason he just hadn't died yet. Berger's PR guy **2.** _____ that Berger had been feeling lousy for the last couple of days."

"So those three were **3.** _____ ..."

"Yeah," Nathan continues. "Pete was pretty amazed at Berger's all round physical **4.** _____ . I mean, this guy has been doing drugs and boozing for years. You've heard about him, right? He used to be quite the man. And then there was a **5.** _____ . I think he was even arrested, I can't remember."

"Okay, you look into that, will you?" asks Daniel. "I mean we are still looking for a motive here. Even if we have found out about the poison, I still have no idea *why* these people were all killed. I mean, do you think it's possible that the person who poisoned all three simply lost his head when Berger just wouldn't die? Maybe that's why Berger was stabbed. We really need to find out if McGraw was also poisoned."

Daniel pauses, turning over possible motives in his head. But he can't think of anything that makes sense.

He turns to Nathan, "I'm going to the hospital to talk to Mr. Dempsey. I dropped Penelope off there earlier. Don't tell the Chief."

Nathan gives Daniel an odd look. He stays quiet for a second.

Daniel notices and asks, "What? Why are you looking at me like that?"

Nathan shakes his head. "So, you don't know?"

"Know what?"

"Well, I don't have a motive yet either. But your British buddies, Penelope and Mr. Dempsey, are not who they say they are."

"Excuse me?"

"Well, it turns out that Mr. Dempsey is not Mr. Dempsey at all. That's just an alias he used as a tax agent to investigate someone here. His real name is Mr. Battersea. And he wasn't investigating anyone. He was here because Ms. Harrington asked him to come. McGraw told me when he asked me to meet him at Lenox. I couldn't tell you before, because Ms. Battersea was in the car with you."

Exercise 54: Questions. Ergänzen Sie das richtige Fragewort!

1. _____ are you looking at me like that?

2. _____ are you going?

3. _____ were these people all killed?

4. _____ about Berger?

5. _____ is behind all this?

Daniel **is dumbfounded**. He tries to say something, but he finds he can't.

"So, what you are saying is…," he stutters.

"What I am saying is that Mr. Dempsey is Penelope's father," says Nathan calmly.

"I don't believe it. No. This can't be true…," Daniel's voice **trails off**.

"Look, Daniel, I'm sorry. But the good news is…"

"Good news? Are you crazy, Nathan? What good news? Three people have been poisoned. I saw one of the victims being stabbed to death yesterday! McGraw was run over when I was standing right next to him, just two hours ago. And now you're telling me that Penelope has been lying to me all along? I mean, I even took her along to Mrs. Carmine. What was I thinking?"

Daniel runs his fingers through his thick hair in frustration.

⚡ buddy	Kumpel
alias	Deckname
to be dumb-founded	sprachlos sein
to trail off	allmählich verstummen
at large	*hier*: auf freiem Fuβ

"Calm down, partner," says Nathan quietly. "We have to keep thinking here. This killer is still **at large**."

Suddenly, Daniel jerks his head up. "Nathan, this ring here was given to Penelope by Ms. Harrington just before she died. It's the same one I found in Mr. Dempsey's, erm, Mr. Battersea's things that you brought from the Café."

Nathan is silent for a moment. "So you think Dempsey, erm Battersea, is behind all this? But he was in hospital when McGraw was killed."

"Yes, he was. But he could be the one with the poison, couldn't he?"

"Maybe. I don't know. We still don't have a motive." Nathan sounds skeptical.

Exercise 55: Questions about the text. Beantworten Sie die Fragen zum Text!

1. Was Mr. Berger poisoned, too?

   _____

2. Mr. Berger was stabbed. Why? What does Daniel think?

   _____

3. Is Daniel upset about Mr. Battersea's real identity?

   _____

4. Why didn't Nathan tell Daniel about Mr. Battersea's identity earlier?

   _____

They sit next to each other in silence for a few moments. Then, Daniel remembers McGraw's envelope. He opens it and lays the content on the table.

It's Ms. Harrington's will and five letters with the same message in cut-out letters:

> **BERGER CAN'T INHERIT.**
> **YOU KNOW WHY. DO SOMETHING!**

"Oh my God!" exclaims Daniel. "Mr. Battersea was blackmailing Ms. Harrington the whole time. He was trying to get Ms. Harrington to change her will. And when that didn't work out, he started poisoning people. McGraw must have found out somehow."

"Hmm. Yes. I'm not sure if…"

"Listen, Nathan, that explains the ring." Daniel's voice is excited. "Penelope told me that Harrington put it in her hand just before she died. She was probably trying to tell Penelope that her father was…"

"You mean, Harrington thought Dempsey, I mean Battersea, had poisoned Duvane?"

Exercise 56: Unscramble. Bilden Sie sinnvolle Wörter aus dem Buchstabenchaos!

1. They sit next to each other in lecisne _____.

2. You need to get to the bottom of the sdanalc

   _____.

3. Penelope's father is in the posiltha _____.

4. Dempsey is the nimisngs _____ link.

5. He welofold _____ us to the hospital.

"Exactly," Daniel nods. "And maybe Battersea poisoned Berger and McGraw, too. I need you to get to the bottom of the scandal surrounding Berger. I still don't know who this hooded figure is, but I'm sure Battersea is the missing link. I need to speak to him and Penelope." His head shoots up. "Oh God, Penelope! I'm such a fool. He probably followed us to the hospital as well…"

"Who? What do you mean?"

But Daniel has already grabbed his keys and is halfway down the hall. He shouts back to Nathan, "The hooded killer. He's probably at the hospital, just waiting for Penelope to come out!"

8 DEATH CAP

Penelope walks out of the hospital room and looks for Daniel's number in her phone.

"Daniel?" she calls after he picks up.

"Penelope? Where are you?"

"I'm still at the hospital. I just spoke to… Listen, Daniel, there are some things that I have to tell you…"

"I know. I'm coming right over. Meet me downstairs in the parking lot. There is some stuff I need to tell you, too."

⚡ to hit sb.	jmd. aufgehen
recently	in letzter Zeit
to fiddle with	herumspielen mit
to dodge	ausweichen
to shift down a gear	einen Gang runterschalten

Penelope walks down the two flights of stairs and out of the hospital. The sun hits her full force, and she searches in her handbag for her sunglasses. Her eyes are so tired. It's a mixture of jet lag, lack of sleep and just too much excitement. As Penelope puts her sunglasses on, her mind goes back to the papers that she found on her father's desk. And then it **hits her**: the word "d. cap" means *Death Cap*, the poisonous mushroom.

Where did I see that word **recently**? she thinks, **fiddling** distractedly **with** her hair.

Of course! Father thinks that Ms. Harrington was poisoned. That would explain why she was having stomach pain on the night she died. The sound of screeching tires blocks Penelope's thoughts. She lifts her head up in surprise.

What's going on? she thinks in a panic as she watches the oncoming car. It is coming straight at her. And Penelope can make out that the driver is wearing a hoodie. Oh God, it's him! The man from the bar. And he is trying to run her down.

Exercise 57: Translation quiz. Übersetzen Sie und enträtseln Sie das Lösungswort!

1. Nummer   __ __ [ ] __ __ __

2. Mischung   __ __ __ [ ] __ __

3. suchen   [ ] __ __ __ __

4. Haar   [ ] __ __ __

5. unten (im Haus)   __ __ __ __ __ __ __ [ ] __

6. Gift   __ [ ] __ [ ] __

7. entgegenkommend   __ __ __ [ ] __ __ __

    Lösung: __ __ __ __ __ __ __

Frantic, Penelope looks left and right to see if there is any way she can dodge the car. She is standing between two rows of cars – the distance to the steps of the hospital is too far. She won't have a chance to avoid getting hit if she tries to run back inside. The car is now about 11 yards away, and she can hear the driver shift down a gear – he is speeding up!

Oh God. What am I going to do?

At the last moment, Penelope jumps between the two cars standing closest to her and falls to the floor. Her hands and elbows explode in pain, and for a second everything around her seems to have become so still.

In that moment, she sees the car running over the spot that she was standing in just seconds ago. Relief spreads through her, and her whole body is shuddering.

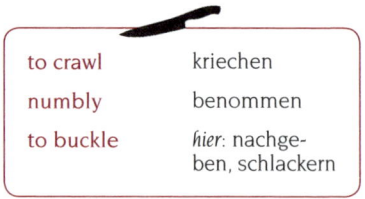

to crawl	kriechen
numbly	benommen
to buckle	*hier*: nachge-ben, schlackern

Still on her elbows, she turns her body around and crawls forward to look where the vehicle is now. Oh no! It's turning and coming toward her again.

Suddenly, Daniel's voice calls out to her. "Penelope, over here."

Numbly, she gets up but has trouble standing because her knees are buckling. On the other side of the cars, Daniel's car has pulled up.

"Get in!" he shouts, holding the door open. "That's him!"

Exercise 58: Infinitive or -ing form? Lesen Sie weiter und ergänzen Sie die passende Verbform!

As fast as she can, Penelope jumps in. Daniel is already

1. accelerate _____, before she has even

climbed into the seat properly. On the other side of the

parking lot, they can **2.** see _____ the car

that just tried **3.** run _____ over Penelope. It

looks as if the driver **4.** wait _____ for some-

thing.

"He hasn't seen me," says Daniel. "He thinks you are still between the cars. Buckle up. We're going **5.** get _____ the bastard now!"

Daniel shifts gears, speeds up again, and they aim toward the other car. Now *they* are the one's driving across the parking lot with screeching tires. The other driver sees them coming, shifts into reverse, does a quick turn, and races out of the parking lot. Daniel turns his own car around and goes after the fleeing vehicle, hard on its heels. The hunt has begun.

"Daniel, what the…?" Penelope manages to ask.

"Hang on tight. This is going to be a bumpy ride."

Daniel puts on his blue light, picks up his car walkie-talkie, and gives

reverse	Rückwärtsgang
hard on sb.'s heels	jmd. dicht auf den Fersen
bumpy	holprig
⚡ to floor it	losrasen

his position to headquarters. "Backup. I need backup. I'm following the suspect in the Berger and McGraw killings. The perp's car is a dark blue Honda Civic convertible. Yes. Follow my position via GPS!" The McGraw killing? Penelope is confused.

Daniel floors it and concentrates on following the dark convertible. Is this really happening? wonders Penelope. Am I really sitting in a police car following a murder suspect? I feel as though I'm going to be sick…

"Penelope, listen, this is the same guy who ran McGraw over at Lenox earlier."

"Lenox?" Penelope has no idea what Daniel is talking about.

"Forget it. McGraw is dead and that guy killed him," shouts Daniel.

"He must have seen me drop you off at the hospital earlier; then he

117

followed me to the mall. After that he came back here to wait for you. Got it?"

Penelope doesn't know what to say to this bizarre situation, so she doesn't answer at all.

Daniel zooms around the next corner at breakneck speed, and Penelope is pushed back into her seat.

"Daniel, there is something you must know…"

"Nathan told me. Dempsey is your father. You don't have to cover for him anymore. Nathan knows everything, too. We're going to get this guy here. And we are going to get your father for blackmail."

"But…"

"Penelope, I realize you had nothing to do with all this. I believe you. You don't have to worry."

⚡ to zoom	rasen
condescend-ing	herablassend
culprit	Täter
⚡ to t-bone	seitlich ram-men
to swerve	ausscheren
split second	Sekunden-bruchteil
median bar-rier	Mittelleit-planke

"Daniel, listen to me!" she shouts, frustrated at his condescending speech. "I'm not worried about myself right now. I'm trying to tell you that my father has nothing to do with this."

"Penelope… wwwooooaaahhh…"

The perp's car has just run over red lights and is taking the fastest way out of Atlanta. They follow at full speed and head toward the interstate highway.

"Daniel!" screeches Penelope.

The police car has a lot more power than the Honda they are following. Two hundred yards down the interstate, Daniel closes in on the convertible. Overhead, Penelope can hear a helicopter. That must be backup.

Daniel looks over into the car at the hooded figure. Who is this guy?

Exercise 59: Synonyms. Lesen Sie weiter und unterstreichen Sie im Text die Synonyme für die folgenden
Wörter!

| to shout | peek | to focus | very fast | beside |

| car |

"Oh my God!" he exclaims and nearly loses control of the

vehicle.

The hood has come off of the **culprit's** head, and Daniel gets

a look at the dark blonde hair. The sunglasses are off and...

"Mrs. Carmine?" Penelope shouts, gasping for breath.

"What?"

The two cars are driving right next to each other, still at full

speed. Mrs. Carmine glances over at them, presses her lips

together and **t-bones** the police car. Taking the hit at that

speed, Daniel's car **swerves** out of control. He slows down

and concentrates on regaining control of his vehicle.

Holding onto the steering wheel with all his strength, Daniel manages to guide his car back into the lane. A **split second** later and
they would have hit the **median barrier** in the middle of the interstate.

Distracted by his maneuvers , Daniel loses sight of Mrs. Carmine's car for just a moment.

"Look!" cries Penelope, pointing at the Honda.

In a **knee-jerk** reaction, Mrs. Carmine has taken the next exit at the last moment. It's too late for Daniel and Penelope to follow.

Achten Sie auf die Rechtschreibung: „Manöver" wird im Britischen **manoeuvre** geschrieben. Gesprochen wird es [mə'nuvər], es reimt sich also auf „hoover".

Daniel hits the steering wheel in frustration and curses loudly.

He takes the walkie-talkie in his hand again. "The perp in the blue Honda convertible has left the highway! I can't follow her. Have the **copter** on her heels. I'm heading for Covington where she lives. I need someone to be there. Ask the local police to wait for us at Mrs. Carmine's house. Nathan has the address."

A moment later, Penelope can hear the helicopter change its course.

Daniel turns to Penelope. "I have no idea what's going on. The hooded killer is Mrs. Carmine? But why? And how's your father involved?"

"My father was helping his old friend, Ms. Harrington," Penelope replies. "Someone was blackmailing her, and he was trying to find out who it was. Then McGraw found out something, but before

knee-jerk	spontan
⚡ **copter**	Heli(kopter)
scientific	wissenschaftlich

he could tell my father about it at the GACC party, Ms. Harrington died, and my father ended up in the hospital. Just now at the hospital he told me that Death Cap has something to do with it. I think my father believes that everyone was being poisoned with Death Cap."

Exercise 60: Questions about the text. Beantworten Sie die Fragen zum Text!

1. When does the Honda driver t-bone Daniel's car?

_____

2. What happens after Daniel's car is hit?

_____

3. Does Daniel follow the car out of the next exit?

_____

4. What does Daniel think the helicopter should do?

_____

5. How do they recognize Mrs. Carmine?

_____

"Death Cap?" asks Daniel. "What's that? Forensics said something about a mushroom. But it was called something scientific... Ama... something."

"Amanita phalloides," whispers Penelope.

That's the word that I saw on one of the drawings in Mrs. Carmine's sitting room, she thinks. Death Cap is also called Amanita Phalloides.

"That's right. That's the word," Daniel replies. He shakes his head in disbelief. "Now, I get it!"

"What do you mean?" asks Penelope.

Exercise 61: Verb forms. Lesen Sie weiter und setzen Sie die korrekte Verbform ein!

"Remember Mrs. Carmine **1. come** _____ out from behind her house?" asks Daniel. "There was something reflecting there. She probably **2. have** _____ a hothouse. That's where she must **3. get** _____ the mushroom from. Mrs. Carmine was blackmailing Ms. Harrington and when that **4. not work** _____, Mrs. Carmine poisoned her," Daniel explains excitedly. "The blackmailing had something to do with Mr. Berger. And when he didn't die of the poison, she **5. kill** _____ him, too."

"Berger was poisoned? By Mrs. Carmine?" Penelope feels **out of her depth**. "But why did Mrs. Carmine come into the bar after she stabbed Mr. Berger? What was she looking for? Me?"
"The ring. Could she have seen Ms. Harrington give it to you?"
"That's it. Mrs. Carmine was standing right next to me."
Now everything is **falling into place**.
"That ring is why I suspected your father," Daniel explains. "You see, I found his ring **among** the things that Nathan brought in after the Berger incident at that Café. I **was convinced** that it was proof that he was blackmailing Ms. Harrington."

They are both quiet for a moment, following the speeding car in front of them.

"Only about two miles, then we're in Covington. Carmine must know that she's cornered. It is the suspects who know that who are the most dangerous. I need you to stay out of sight when we get there, okay?" says Daniel strictly in his detective voice.

Penelope nods. "Hmm, sure. You said Mrs. Carmine killed McGraw, too? That's terrible. But why?"

"Money? Revenge? I don't know yet. And I still don't have a motive…"

They are interrupted as Daniel's cell phone rings.

"Nathan?" calls Daniel when his colleague's number pops up on the display. "You're on the hands-free. Penelope is here."

"Ah, yes. Listen, Daniel, head-quarters just told me that you are on your way to Carmine's and following her. I've found out some stuff about this woman. Don't do anything until backup has arrived, okay?"

out of one's depth	überfordert, ins Schwimmen geraten
to fall into place	einen Sinn ergeben
among	unter, inmitten
to be convinced	überzeugt sein
cornered	in die Enge getrieben
revenge	Rache
underage	minderjährig

"Fine. But what did you find out?" asks Daniel.

"Carmine is actually her maiden name," answers Nathan.

Penelope nods and Daniel raises an eyebrow at her.

"My father just told me," she explains.

"Anyway," Nathan continues, "17 years ago she was in the hospital as a Mrs. Coughlin, giving birth to her second child, when her husband and three-year-old daughter were hit and killed by an underage drunk driver. Guess who that was?"

"Tommy Berger," whisper Penelope and Daniel at the same time.

Exercise 62: Fill in the blanks. Lesen Sie weiter und setzen Sie die Begriffe richtig ein!

lawyer	nephew	born	years	answer

money	by chance

"Yeah. Awful story," says Nathan. "Husband and child both dead. Then Mrs. Coughlin's, **aka** Mrs. Carmine's, baby died right after it was **1.** _____ . Berger was never **convicted** because he had the best **legal defense** **2.** _____ can buy. Guess who?"

"McGraw!" Penelope and Daniel **3.** _____ at the same time again.

"Very good," Nathan replies. "McGrow defended Berger in court. And now for the grande horrible finale: Ms. Harrington paid his **4.** _____ , McGraw. She was Berger's aunt, and he was always her favorite **5.** _____ . It seems Carmine met them all again **6.** _____ later **7.** _____ when she joined the Junior League Horticultural Society."

"It must have been a shock for her when she found out that her friend, Judy Harrington, was actually the person supporting the man who had killed her entire family!" Daniel continues.

"That's why Berger was so **distressed** that night at the GACC function when he saw Mrs. Carmine there. He must have recognized her," says Penelope.

"Yeah," Daniel agrees and **deduces** from the information he has what has happened. "When Mrs. Carmine found out who Harrington's beneficiary was, she must have gone crazy. It must have been a nightmare for her to see this man go free, living the easy life. That must have been the last straw for her. I'm guessing Duvane was an accident. He was just in the wrong place at the wrong time."

Daniel clears his throat. Now he is in his element. "And Carmine could have poisoned them all at any earlier Junior League functions. There's an event every week, isn't there? Nathan, check out how much of this mushroom is needed for it to be **fatal**. I'm sure you only need a little bit, and it probably wasn't a problem for Carmine to mix it into a drink or the hors d'oeuvres that people have at these events."

aka (also known as)	alias
to convict	verurteilen
legal defense	Rechtsbeistand
distressed	erschüttert
to deduce	schlussfolgern
fatal	tödlich

"What you're saying really adds up, Dan. You be careful now. We'll talk later at the station," Nathan says just before he hangs up after a short pause.

Ten minutes later, Daniel and Penelope arrive at Mrs. Carmine's driveway. They hear the sound of the helicopter overhead. The requested police backup hasn't arrived yet.

So I was right. She headed home, Daniel thinks.

He is on full alert; his heart is pounding in anticipation of a show-down.

Penelope holds her breath. What is going to happen now? Where is Mrs. Carmine?

The sound coming from behind them surprises him. It's the Honda. From out of nowhere, it speeds past them, heading straight for the house. Penelope can't believe her eyes. Is Mrs. Carmine really driving toward the house at full speed?

Penelope feels her stomach lurch as the sickening sound of the car hitting the walls of the house reaches her. The explosion that follows is deafening. The Honda seems suspended in midair for a moment before it comes down with an earsplitting crash on the hothouse behind the house. As if the world turns into a million re-

pounding	pochen, häm-mern
anticipation	Erwartung
to lurch	*hier*: sich ver-krampfen
deafening	ohrenbetäu-bend
suspended in midair	in der Luft hängend
earsplitting	ohrenbetäu-bend

flecting shards, the scene is beautiful and terrible at the same time.

Penelope looks on in horror. Part of the hood of Mrs. Carmine's car is stuck in the wall of the hothouse; the rest is going up in flames in the wall of her home.

Penelope and Daniel both get out of the car at the same time and run toward the burning car as fast as they can.

Penelope feels her skin singe from the heat of the flames as she gets closer. Mrs. Carmine has opened the car door and is crawling toward them. Her face and hair are blood-smeared; the look in her eyes is frantic.

"Mrs. Carmine, get away from here," shouts Penelope.

She grabs Mrs. Carmine arms, and Daniel is by their side in a moment. In a joint effort, they drag Mrs. Carmine to her feet and start to move away from the burning car.

shards *pl*	Glasscherben
to singe	versengen
joint effort	gemeinsame Anstrengung
pleading	flehend
to hover	schweben

Mrs. Carmine's face is only a few inches from Penelope's ear, so Penelope can hear her clearly, although her voice is no more than a whisper.

"Ms. Battersea, I'm sorry," her voice is pleading. "It was never about you. I just couldn't let Tommy get it all, when I have nothing. I…"

"Mrs. Carmine…," interrupts Penelope.

"No, please listen. I… Judy told me about her will – I just couldn't live with that. I wanted everyone to feel the hurt I have felt. And now…"

Her voice dies away.

Penelope looks down at Mrs. Carmine, whose eyes have closed.

Mrs. Coughlin's car is still burning, and the house has caught on fire. The police helicopter is hovering overhead. Backup police sirens are getting louder as more police officers arrive at the scene. Mrs. Coughlin has gotten her revenge. And her life has come full circle at the place where she had once been so happy. But some wrongs can never really be made right again.

Bewildered, Penelope wipes her teary eyes and nervously looks over to Daniel. Daniel extends his arms to give her a warm, tender embrace.

to come full circle	der Kreis schließt sich
tender	zärtlich

FINAL TEST

Exercise 1: Word spiral. Finden Sie die Begriffe in der Wortspirale!

1	2	3	4	5	6	7
22	23	24	25	26	27	8
21	36	37	38	39	28	9
20	35	42	41	40	29	10
19	34	33	32	31	30	11
18	17	16	15	14	13	12

1-9: word for investigative police officer in the US

9-16: proof of guilt in police investigation

16-22: synonym for "shout"

22-27: synonym for "shared" in the context of interest

27-33: the level part at the bottom or top if a staircase

33-42: successful completion of studies

Exercise 2: Negatives. Verneinen Sie die folgenden Sätze!

1. Why is Penelope worried about her father?

   _____

2. I really understand what's going on.

   _____

3. Nathan has figured out who Penelope's father is.

   _____

4. Daniel can take Penelope to the hospital, can't he?

   _____

5. Penelope went to Mrs. Carmine's house with Daniel.

   _____

Exercise 3: Idiomatic expressions. Welche Ausdrücke haben dieselbe Bedeutung?

1. ☐ Got it?		a) Pleased to meet you.
2. ☐ No buts about it.		b) Did you understand?
3. ☐ The pleasure's all mine.		c) I have to check.
4. ☐ Hold on, let me see.		d) Fasten your seatbelt.
5. ☐ Buckle up.		e) I won't take no for an answer.

Exercise 4: Questions about the text. Beantworten Sie die Fragen zum Text!

1. Why did Ms. Harrington ask Penelope's father to help her?

   _____

2. What does Penelope think when Ms. Harrington gives her the ring?

   _____

3. Where does Penelope meet Daniel for the first time?

   _____

4. How does Penelope find out what d. cap means?

   _____

5. When does Daniel suspect Penelope's father?

   _____

Exercise 5: Word forms. Ergänzen Sie das jeweilige Substantiv und Adverb!

1. weak   _____   _____

2. exciting   _____   _____

3. unconscious   _____   _____

4. angry   _____   _____

5. strong   _____   _____

Exercise 6: True or false? Kreuzen Sie die richtigen Aussagen an!

1. Nathan is worried about his partner's behavior. ❐

2. Penelope has known Ms. Harrington her whole life. ❐

3. Ms. Harrington is surprised when Penelope calls. ❐

4. Nathan finds out who Mrs. Carmine really is. ❐

5. The hooded killer doesn't attack Penelope's father. ❐

6. Daniel has worked with Mr. Dempsey before. ❐

Exercise 7: Anglicisms. Geben Sie die amerikanische Entsprechung der britischen Begriffe an!

1. motorway _____

2. lift _____

3. colour _____

4. to ring sb. _____

5. town centre _____

6. casualty department _____

7. petrol _____

8. favourite _____

9. pavement _____

ANSWERS

Exercise 1:   **1.** c **2.** a **3.** d **4.** b

Exercise 2:   **1.** orchid **2.** valuable **3.** message **4.** beautiful **5.** Penelope **6.** emergency

Exercise 3:   **1.** No, her father doesn't have many friends.
2. No, they have never met before.
3. Penelope is British.
4. Her father is a horticulturalist.

Exercise 4:   **1.** brought, brought **2.** left, left **3.** knew, known **4.** thought, thought **5.** saw, seen

Exercise 5:   **1.** b **2.** b **3.** a **4.** b

Exercise 6:   **1.** small **2.** athletic **3.** thoughtful **4.** old-fashioned **5.** better **6.** outward **7.** attractive

Exercise 7:   **1.** purse **2.** realize **3.** cell phone **4.** center **5.** neighbor

Exercise 8:   **Across:** stopover, lounge, jetlag, transfer
Down: plane, hotel

Exercise 9:   **1.** knock **2.** voice **3.** breakfast **4.** shower **5.** staircase **6.** kitchen

Exercise 10:   **1.** women **2.** children **3.** disappearances **4.** doors **5.** voices

Exercise 11:   **1.** She can feel her heart pounding.
2. I wish I could find my father.
3. She hands Penelope her coffee.
4. She knew him well.

Exercise 12:   **1.** true **2.** false (She doesn't know where he is.)
3. true **4.** false (She has to go straight away.)
5. false (She puts it in her pocket.)

Exercise 13: 1. She is left sitting alone in the room.
2. Her thoughts are interrupted.
3. He reminds Penelope of Keanu Reeves.
4. Penelope folds them.
5. They are wonderfully green.

Exercise 14: 1. lady 2. precinct 3. reflection 4. witness 5. cop
6. question 7. different 8. unbelievable 9. gentle
Lösung: detective

Exercise 15: 1. was 2. show 3. was 4. asked 5. found 6. breathing

Exercise 16: 1. d 2. c 3. a 4. e 5. b

Exercise 17: 1. true 2. false (She doesn't understand.) 3. false
(He has met him before.) 4. true

Exercise 18: 1. c 2. a 3. d 4. b

Exercise 19: 1. I don't have any American money.
2. I myself haven't ever met an unfriendly British person.
3. You've known Mr. Dempsey for a long time then?
4. This won't help the investigation.

Exercise 20: 1. a, d, e 2. b, c, f

Exercise 21: 1. happy 2. mansion 3. truth 4. disappearance
5. idyllic

Exercise 22: 1. eyes 2. enough 3. figure 4. breaks 5. gloves
6. freezes

Exercise 23: 1. sitting 2. holding 3. watches 4. struggling 5. come

Exercise 24: **Across:** 1. chief 4. cop 5. detective 7. stopover
Down: 2. hoodie 3. investigate 5. dead 6. murder

Exercise 25: 1. d 2. c 3. a 4. e 5. b

Exercise 26: 1. break 2. surprised 3. meet 4. look 5. know

Exercise 27: 1. quietly 2. forcefully 3. important 4. soft 5. extremely happy

Exercise 28: 1. false (He takes Penelope to the bar.) 2. true
3. true 4. true

Exercise 29: **1.** c **2.** e **3.** a **4.** b **5.** d

Exercise 30: **1.** Pete didn't text me that Mr. Duvane had a liver condition.
2. Daniel doesn't interrupt her thoughts.
3. I don't remember Mrs. Carmine from the party last night.
4. You didn't go straight to the GACC fund-raiser.
5. I don't remember!

Exercise 31: **1.** link **2.** party **3.** morning **4.** list **5.** time **6.** police station

Exercise 32:

1 G	2 O	3 V	4 E	5 R	6 N
20 V	21 A	22 T	23 O	24 R	7 M
19 E	32 S	33 T	34 A	25 E	8 E
18 L	31 M	36 E	35 R	26 S	9 N
17 E	30 O	29 O	28 R	27 T	10 T
16 P	15 O	14 H	13 T	12 U	11 R

Exercise 33: **1.** c **2.** e **3.** f **4.** a **5.** b **6.** d

Exercise 34: **1.** is **2.** has taken **3.** followed **4.** is **5.** had calmed **6.** to get

Exercise 35: **1.** Yes, she recognized a few of his physical attributes.
2. No, he decided to take her out for drinks.
3. It's important because now both attacks are connected to one another.
4. It worries her a lot.
5. No, she is not sure of them at all.

Exercise 36: **1.** the room's light switches **2.** her father's lists **3.** her father's favorite pens **4.** the bedroom's doors **5.** the graduate's faces

Exercise 37: 1. Sie kennen sich seit dem College.
2. Er trägt den Ring an seinem rechten Zeigefinger.
3. Er hat so getan, als würde er seine Tochter nicht kennen.
4. Das Blatt liegt halb versteckt unter dem Bücherstapel.
5. Die Notiz besteht aus einzelnen Buchstaben.
6. Vielleicht hat er etwas Schreckliches getan.

Exercise 38: 1. he 2. You 3. I 4. my 5. me 6. his

Exercise 39: 1. suddenly 2. possibly 3. strong 4. slight 5. tall 6. well

Exercise 40: 1. plants 2. thought 3. stab 4. poison 5. detective
6. suspect 7. kidney 8. investigation 9. connection
Lösung: suspicion

Exercise 41: 1. way 2. witness 3. notes 4. voice 5. investigation
6. answers

Exercise 42: 1. says 2. earlier 3. confused 4. happened 5. night
6. things

Exercise 43: 1. d 2. e 3. f 4. a 5. c 6. b

Exercise 44: 1. sunglasses 2. voice 3. crying 4. death 5. glasses

Exercise 45: 1. He asks where she was exactly when she died.
2. She says that she can't believe that she's really gone.
3. She asks him why he's asking.
4. She asks them to excuse her for leaving her sunglasses on.

Exercise 46: 1. Penelope is upset.
2. I landed in Atlanta the day before yesterday.
3. He is very patient with her.
4. She has a bad conscience.
5. Listen, I'm only doing my job.

Exercise 47: 1. false (Daniel realizes that he is in trouble.) 2. true
3. false (He can go there.) 4. false (She is looking for answers.) 5. false (He calls Daniel on the phone.)

Exercise 48: **Across:** suit, breakneck, siren
Down: frantic, speed, unnatural, hood, rogue

Exercise 49:

1 H	2 O	3 S	4 P	5 I	6 T
20 H	21 T	22 E	23 R	24 E	7 A
19 G	32 N	33 T	34 E	25 C	8 L
18 U	31 E	36 S	35 R	26 O	9 I
17 A	30 Z	29 I	28 N	27 G	10 E
16 D	15 E	14 T	13 I	12 C	11 X

Exercise 50: 1. to 2. to 3. too 4. to 5. to 6. too

Exercise 51: 1. mirror 2. hours 3. paramedics 4. crime scene 5. deaths

Exercise 52: 1. exhausted, more exhausted 2. deeper, deepest 3. stern, sternest 4. more stunned, most stunned 5. more amazed, most amazed

Exercise 53: 1. interesting 2. confirmed 3. poisoned 4. fitness 5. scandal

Exercise 54: 1. Why 2. Where 3. Why 4. What 5. Who

Exercise 55: 1. Yes, he was poisoned as well.
2. Daniel thinks that someone might have just lost his head because Mr. Berger did not die as quickly as the others.
3. Yes, because he realizes that Penelope has been lying to him all along.
4. Nathan didn't tell him, because Penelope was in the car with Daniel.

Exercise 56: 1. silence 2. scandal 3. hospital 4. missing 5. followed

Exercise 57: 1. number 2. mixture 3. search 4. hair 5. downstairs 6. poison 7. oncoming
Lösung: mushroom

Exercise 58: 1. accelerating 2. see 3. to run 4. is waiting 5. to get

Exercise 59: 1. exclaims 2. vehicle 3. look 4. next to 5. at full speed 6. concentrates

Exercise 60: **1.** The driver t-bones Daniel's car when Daniel drives next to it.
2. His car swerves, and it nearly hits the safety barrier.
3. He was distracted and now can't get off at the exit; it's too late.
4. The helicopter should follow Mrs. Carmine.
5. Her hood has come off.

Exercise 61: **1.** came **2.** has **3.** have gotten **4.** didn't work **5.** killed

Exercise 62: **1.** born **2.** money **3.** answer **4.** lawyer **5.** nephew **6.** years **7.** by chance

Exercise 63: **1.** d **2.** e **3.** a **4.** c **5.** b

FINAL TEST

Exercise 1:

1 D	2 E	3 T	4 E	5 C	6 T	7 I
22 M	23 U	24 T	25 U	26 A	27 L	8 V
21 I	36 D	37 U	38 A	39 T	28 A	9 E
20 A	35 A	42 N	41 O	40 I	29 N	10 V
19 L	34 R	33 G	32 N	31 I	30 D	11 I
18 C	17 X	16 E	15 C	14 N	13 E	12 D

Exercise 2: **1.** Why isn't Penelope worried about her father?
2. I really don't understand what's going on.
3. Nathan hasn't figured out who Penelope's father is.
4. Daniel cannot/can't take Penelope to the hospital, can he?
5. Penelope did not/didn't go to Mrs. Carmine's house with Daniel.

Exercise 3: 1. b 2. e 3. a 4. c 5. d

Exercise 4: 1. She didn't want to involve the police.
2. She is worried that her father is in trouble.
3. Penelope meets Daniel at the police station for the first time.
4. She remembers what it means when she thinks back to the note she found on her father's desk.
5. Daniel suspects Penelope's father when he finds her father's ring.

Exercise 5: 1. weakness, weakly 2. excitement, excitedly 3. unconsciousness, unconsciously 4. anger, angrily 5. strength, strongly

Exercise 6: 1. true 2. false (She has just met her.) 3. false (She seems to have expected her call.) 4. true 5. true 6. true

Exercise 7: 1. highway/expressway 2. elevator 3. color 4. to call sb. 5. downtown 6. emergency room 7. gas/gasoline 8. favorite 9. sidewalk

GLOSSARY

↯ = umgangssprachlich
pl = Plural
UK = britisches Englisch
US = amerikanisches Englisch

absently	geistesabwesend
to accelerate	beschleunigen
↯ to add up	einen Sinn ergeben
agitated	aufgebracht
air	*hier*: Ausstrahlung
aka (also known as)	alias
alias	Deckname
almond-shaped	mandelförmig
Amanita phalloides	Grüner Knollenblätterpilz
among	unter, inmitten
angle	Winkel
annual	jährlich
anticipation	Erwartung
apologetic	entschuldigend
arch	*hier*: Brückenbogen
ASAP (as soon as possible)	schnellstmöglich
asparagus	Spargel
to assess	schätzen, beurteilen
at large	*hier*: auf freiem Fuß
at the top of his voice	so laut er kann
attire	Kleidung, Aufzug

award-winning	preisgekrönt
bad conscience	schlechtes Gewissen
bald	kahlköpfig
bank	*hier*: Ufer
to be convinced	überzeugt sein
to be dumbfounded	sprachlos sein
to be flattered	sich geschmeichelt fühlen
to be in overdrive	auf Hochtouren laufen
beneficiary	Begünstigte(r)
to be poisoned	vergiftet werden
to be quite the man	ein richtiger A-Promi sein
bewildered	verwirrt, verblüfft
to blackmail	erpressen
⚡ bobby *UK*	(Streifen-)Polizist(in)
boozing	Saufen
bouncy	federnd
⚡ breakneck speed	Höllentempo
to buckle	*hier*: nachgeben, schlackern
⚡ buddy	Kumpel
build	Statur
bumpy	holprig
by the book	nach Vorschrift
⚡ to call it a day	(für heute) Schluss machen
carotid artery	Halsschlagader
child abuse	Kindesmisshandlung
⚡ chile *US Dialekt*	Kind
city hall	Rathaus
civil servant	öffentliche(r) Angestellte(r)
class ring	Absolventenring
to clear one's throat	sich räuspern
to clench sth.	etw. (fest) umklammern
to cloud sb.'s judgement	jds. Urteil trüben
clue	Hinweis

coincidence	Zufall
⚡ to come clean	reinen Tisch machen
to come full circle	der Kreis schließt sich
complexion	Teint
concussion	Gehirnerschütterung
condescending	herablassend
to confirm	bestätigen
contaminated	verunreinigt
convertible	Cabrio
to convict	verurteilen
⚡ copter	Heli(kopter)
cornered	in die Enge getrieben
coroner	Gerichtsmediziner(in)
to cover for sb.	jds. Arbeit übernehmen; jmd. decken
cranberry fizz	Longdrink mit Cranberrysaft
⚡ crap device	schrottiges Gerät
to crawl	kriechen
to cringe	(zusammen)zucken
⚡ to cruise	*hier*: entspannt herumfahren
crumpled	*hier*: zerquetscht
cubicle	Box in einem Großraumbüro
culprit	Täter(in)
curb	Bordstein
current	*hier*: aktuell
to curse	fluchen
cutting-edge	supermodern
to dash sb.'s hopes	jds. Hoffnungen zunichtemachen
davenport	Sekretär
deafening	ohrenbetäubend
to deduce	schlussfolgern
desperately	verzweifelt
to detect	entdecken, wahrnehmen

diarrhea	Durchfall
distracted	abgelenkt
distress	Leid, Schmerz
distressed	erschüttert
to dodge	ausweichen
down	*hier*: entfernt von
to drain	*hier*: aufzehren
drawl	gedehnte Sprechweise, hörbarer Akzent
dreadful	fürchterlich
dresser	Kommode
earsplitting	ohrenbetäubend
to eavesdrop	(heimlich) lauschen
elderly	ältere(r)
engraving	*hier*: Stahlstich
engulfed	umringt
entire	gesamte(r,s)
ESTA (Electronic System for Travel Authorisation)	Elektronisches Reisegenehmigungssystem der USA
evidence	Beweis(e)
exhausted	erschöpft
expectantly	erwartungsvoll
expressway *US*	Schnellstraße, Autobahn
facial features *pl*	Gesichtszüge
failure	Versagen
to faint	ohnmächtig werden
to fall apart	*hier*: (psychisch) zusammenbrechen
to fall into place	einen Sinn ergeben
fancy-looking	schick
far-fetched	weit hergeholt
fatal	tödlich
to feel awkward	sich unbehaglich fühlen
to fiddle with	herumspielen mit

fierce	*hier*: grimmig
to fill sb. in	jmd. informieren
flailing	fuchtelnd
flatly	*hier*: ausdruckslos
to flick	*hier*: aufschnappen lassen
to flick on	anknipsen
flight attendant	Steward(ess)
to flip through sth.	etw. (schnell) durchblättern
⚡ to floor it	losrasen
frail	gebrechlich, schwach
frantically	verzweifelt, wie wild
fraternizing	*hier*: unprofessionelle Nähe erlauben
to freeze (froze, frozen)	*hier*: erstarren (lassen)
frozen	*hier*: erstarrt
GACC (German American Chamber of Commerce)	Deutsch-Amerikanische Handelskammer
to gasp for breath	nach Luft schnappen
gaze	Blick
gesture	Geste
to get a lead	einen Hinweis bekommen
to give sth. a go	etw. (mal) probieren
to glance	blicken
to glimpse	flüchtig erblicken
to go about sth.	etw. angehen
government	Regierung
to go weak in the knees	weiche Knie bekommen
to grab	ergreifen
to graduate	einen akademischen Abschluss erwerben
gruesome	schaurig
to grunt	grummeln, grunzen
to gush	*hier*: hervorströmen
hard on sb.'s heels	jmd. dicht auf den Fersen

head nurse *US*	leitende Stationsschwester
heading	Überschrift
headquarters	Zentrale
to head toward	auf etw. zusteuern
heart-piercing	markerschütternd
hesitantly	zögerlich
highlighted	hervorgehoben
high-rise	Hochhaus
⚡ to hit (hit, hit) **sb.**	jmd. aufgehen
HMRC (Her Majesty's Revenue and Customs)	britische Steuerbehörde
⚡ hollerin'	Brüllen
to honk	hupen
⚡ mike	Mikro
hood *US*	Motorhaube; Kapuze
hoodie	Kapuzenpullover
horn-rimmed glasses	Hornbrille
horrific	entsetzlich
horticultural	Gartenbau…
hothouse	Gewächshaus
to hover	schweben
hunch	Ahnung, Gefühl
to hurtle	sausen, schleudern
⚡ I'll have none of it.	Davon will ich nichts wissen.
impeccably groomed	tadellos gepflegt
in disgust	entrüstet
incident	Vorfall, Ereignis
incredible	unglaublich
incredulously	ungläubig
index finger	Zeigefinger
to inherit	erben
⚡ in no taam *US* (*Dialekt*)	sofort
insecure	unsicher

to insist	bestehen auf
interrogation room	Verhörraum
intimate	intim, vertraut
intrigued	fasziniert
intruder	Eindringling
investigating	ermittelnd
irritated	ärgerlich
IRS (Internal Revenue Service)	US Steuerbehörde
to jerk	(sich) ruckartig bewegen
jet-black	pechschwarz
joint effort	gemeinsame Anstrengung
joint	*hier*: Schuppen, Spelunke
jolt	*hier*: Schock
to keep sth. in check	etw. unter Kontrolle halten
kettle	Wasserkocher
kidney	Niere
knee-jerk	spontan
ladyfriend	weibliche Bekannte
landing	Treppenabsatz
to latch on	hängenbleiben an
lawyer	Rechtsanwalt/-anwältin
legal defense	Rechtsbeistand
to linger	hängen, verbleiben; nachklingen
literally	tatsächlich, wirklich
liver condition	Leberkrankheit
longish	ziemlich lang
to look sb. over	jmd. mustern
looks *pl*	Aussehen
loose ends *pl*	offene Fragen
lousy	mies
lovebirds *pl*	Turteltauben
to lunge	einen Satz machen

to lurch	*hier*: sich verkrampfen
maid	Hausangestellte
maiden name	Geburtsname
to make a mental note to…	versuchen, daran zu denken zu …
to make out	*hier*: erkennen, ausmachen
mansion	Villa
median barrier	Mittelleitplanke
medical examiner	Gerichtsmediziner(in)
metropolitan	großstädtisch
to mill about	umherlaufen
missing link	fehlendes Bindeglied
modus operandi	Vorgehensweise
to monitor	überwachen
to motion	bedeuten, winken
mutual attraction	gegenseitige Anziehung
nightcap	Absacker
nightmare	Albtraum
⚡ no buts about it	da gibt es kein Wenn und Aber
numbly	benommen
⚡ nutty	verrückt, spleenig
on the other hand…	andererseits …
on the right track	auf der richtigen Spur
orchid	Orchidee
organ failure	Organversagen
out of one's depth	überfordert, ins Schwimmen geraten
pained	gequält
pale	blass
paramedic	Sanitäter(in)
to peer	spähen, schauen
penetrating	eindringlich
pensive	nachdenklich
⚡ perp	Täter(in)
persona	Persönlichkeit, Identität

piece of advice	Ratschlag
piercing	stechend, durchdringend
pillar	Säule
pleading	flehend
plump	pummelig
potting soil	Blumenerde
pounding	pochen, hämmern
precinct	Polizeiwache
predator	Raubtier
prejudice	Vorurteil
preliminary forensic report	vorläufiger rechtsmedizinischer Bericht
presence	Anwesenheit
to pretend	vortäuschen
prey	Beute
private	*hier*: zurückhaltend
properly	vernünftig
to pull up	*hier*: heranziehen
purse *US*	Handtasche
puzzled	verwundert
quaint	idyllisch
rearview mirror	Rückspiegel
reassuring(ly)	beruhigend
recently	in letzter Zeit
reflection	*hier*: Nachdenken
to regain one's composure	seine Fassung wiedergewinnen
to register	*hier*: merken
relief	Erleichterung
relieved	erleichtert
to resuscitate	wiederbeleben
revenge	Rache
reverse	Rückwärtsgang
to revive	(wieder)beleben

revolving door	Drehtür
rib cage	Brustkorb
rocker	*hier*: Kufe
rocking chair	Schaukelstuhl
rogue driver	Amokfahrer(in)
rugged	markant, rau
to run for cover	in Deckung gehen
⚡ satnav	Navi
sb. can't help but...	jmd. muss einfach ...
scattered	*hier*: wirr
scene	*hier*: Tatort
scientific	wissenschaftlich
to scowl	finster/mürrisch blicken
scrape	Schramme, Kratzer
screeching tires *pl*	quietschende Reifen
screen	*hier*: Trennscheibe
to seep	*hier*: schwinden
to send shivers down sb.'s spine	jmd. einen Schauer den Rücken runterlaufen lassen
shards *pl*	Glasscherben
sheepishly	verlegen, beschämt
to shift down a gear	einen Gang runterschalten
to shift position	die Position verändern
⚡ shoot	Scheibenkleister
sickening	entsetzlich
sidewalk *US*	Bürgersteig
signature	*hier*: unverkennbar
to singe	versengen
sip	Schluck
to soak up	aufsaugen
soft	*hier*: träge
softly	*hier*: ruhig, leise
sophisticated	kultiviert

to sort sth. out	etw. regeln
Southern	*hier*: aus den Südstaaten der USA
specifics *pl*	Einzelheiten
speechless	sprachlos
split second	Sekundenbruchteil
spooky	unheimlich
to spot	sehen, erkennen
to spurt	spritzen
to squint	blinzeln
to stab	(zu)stechen
stage name	Künstlername
stain	Fleck
standard procedure	übliches Vorgehen
statement	*hier*: Zeugenaussage
to steer	steuern, lenken
stern	streng
stitch	Stich
stopover	Zwischenstopp
strain	Belastung, Strapazen
to strike (struck, struck) sb. as...	jmd. … erscheinen
striking	auffallend
to stumble	stolpern
stunned	fassungslos, geschockt
to stutter	stottern
to suppose	annehmen, vermuten
supposedly	angeblich
suspect	Verdächtige(r)
suspended in midair	in der Luft hängend
suspicious	verdächtig
to sweep (swept, swept)	fegen
to swerve	ausscheren
swift	schnell, flink

to take sb. into your confidence	jmd. Vertrauen schenken
to take sb. on	es mit jmd. aufnehmen
tangled	verheddert
target	Ziel(scheibe)
tax agent	Steuerbeamte(r)
tax evader	Steuerhinterzieher(in)
⚡ to t-bone	seitlich rammen
tender	zärtlich
terrified	verängstigt
to text	*hier*: SMS schreiben
thud	dumpfer Schlag
toddler	Kleinkind
to the core	bis ins Mark
town council	Stadtrat
to trail off	allmählich verstummen
train of thoughts	Gedankengang
to tremble	zittern
to trickle	tropfen
to tune	stimmen (ein Instrument)
UCLA (University of California, Los Angeles)	Universität von Kalifornien
unconsciously	unbewusst
underage	minderjährig
valid	gültig
valuable	wertvoll, kostbar
vastness	unermessliche Weite
vending machine	Getränkeautomat
vicious	heimtückisch, schrecklich
victim	Opfer
vomiting	Erbrechen
vowel	Vokal
ward	Station im Krankenhaus

ward round	Visite
wariness	Wachsamkeit, Vorsicht
well-to-do	gut situiert
What on earth…?	Was um Himmels willen …?
whereabouts *pl*	Aufenthaltsort
to whip around	herumschnellen
will	*hier*: Testament
to wince	zusammenzucken
to wink	zwinkern
⚡ wiped out	fertig, geschlaucht
with a twinkle in one's eye	mit einem Augenzwinkern
witness	Zeuge/Zeugin
worn-out	erschöpft
wound up	*hier*: aufgedreht
wreck	Wrack
⚡ Ya hear?	Verstehst du?
⚡ to yank	ruckartig ziehen
ziplock bag	wiederverschließbarer Plastik-beutel
⚡ to zoom	rasen

LIST OF EXERCISES

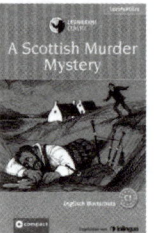

Compact Lernkrimi
Classic

Compact Lernkrimi
Kurzkrimis

Compact Lernkrimi
Lernthriller

Compact Lernkrimi Kurzkrimis	Compact Lernkrimi Lernthriller	
		A1
Blood and Breakfast ISBN 978-3-8174-7760-9 **Deadly Business** ISBN 978-3-8174-9215-2 **Endstation Waterloo Bridge** ISBN 978-3-8174-7733-3 **Es war Mord, my Lord** ISBN 978-3-8174-7734-0 **Mord at Teatime** ISBN 978-3-8174-7839-2		**A2**
Bullets over Bristol ISBN 978-3-8174-8544-4 **Death Comes Knocking** ISBN 978-3-8174-7945-0	**Faceless Killer** ISBN 978-3-8174-8856-8	**B1**
	In Terror ISBN 978-3-8174-8857-5	**B2**
		C1/C2

Compact Lernkrimi
Rätselblock

Compact Lernkrimi
Hörbuch

	Compact Lernkrimi Rätselblock	Compact Lernkrimi Hörbuch
A1		
A2	**The Art of Crime** ISBN 978-3-8174-9155-1	**A Shot in the Night** ISBN 978-3-8174-8202-3 **Death Wish** ISBN 978-3-8174-8204-7 **The Butterworth Mystery** ISBN 978-3-8174-8203-0
B1	**A Deadly Puzzle** ISBN 978-3-8174-8832-2	**Bloody Revenge** ISBN 978-3-8174-8860-5 **Das Mädchen von King's Cross** ISBN 978-3-8174-7673-2 **Der Themse-Mörder** ISBN 978-3-8174-7674-9
B2		**Blutige Erbschaft** ISBN 978-3-8174-7676-3 **Die Intrigantin** ISBN 978-3-8174-7675-6 **Business English** **Mord im Office** ISBN 978-3-8174-7747-0
C1/C2		

Compact Lernkrimi
Audio-Learning

Compact Lernkrimi
Sprachkurs

	Englisch für Anfänger (A1/A2) ISBN 978-3-8174-7784-5	**A1**
Verschollen im Dartmoor ISBN 978-3-8174-7796-8		**A2**
Totenstille im Hyde Park ISBN 978-3-8174-7797-5		**B1**
		B2
		C1/C2